The Triangular Connection:
America, Israel, and American Jews

Latin America and the Palestine Problem
Straddling the Isthmus of Tehuantepec
Peaceful Conflict
Soldiers, Scholars, and Society
Between Israel and Death
Israel and Her Army

The Triangular Connection: America, Israel, and American Jews

EDWARD BERNARD GLICK

London
GEORGE ALLEN & UNWIN
Boston   Sydney

George Allen & Unwin (Publishers) Ltd,
40 Museum Street, London WC1A 1LU, UK

George Allen & Unwin (Publishers) Ltd,
Park Lane, Hemel Hempstead, Herts HP2 4TE, UK

Allen & Unwin, Inc.,
9 Winchester Terrace, Winchester, Mass. 01890, USA

George Allen & Unwin Australia Pty Ltd,
8 Napier Street, North Sydney, NSW 2060, Australia

First published in 1982

British Library Cataloguing in Publication Data

Glick, Edward Bernard
    The triangular connection : America, Israel, and
    American Jews.
    1. Zionism–History
    2. Israel–Foreign relations–United States
    3. United States–Foreign relations–Israel
    I. Title
    956.94'001   DS149
    ISBN 0–04–353008–7

Library of Congress Cataloging in Publication Data

Glick, Edward Bernard
    The Triangular Connection
    Bibliography : P.
    Includes Index.
    1. Zionism–United States. 2. Bible–Prophecies–Jews.
    3. Israel and the Diaspora. 4. Jews–United States–
    politics and government. 5. Jewish–Arab relations.
    6. United States–Foreign relations–Israel. 7. Israel–
    Foreign relations–United States.
    I. Title.
    DS149.G5326   956.94'001   82–6700
    ISBN 0–04–353008–7   AACR2

Set in 11 on 12 point Baskerville by Grove Graphics, Tring
and printed in Great Britain
by Richard Clay (The Chaucer Press) Ltd, Bungay, Suffolk

TO IRA BAND, PHYLLIS BRAVERMAN,
AND MELVIN GLICK

Contents

Acknowledgments   *page* 11
1 Introduction   15

PART ONE   THE HISTORICAL SETTING
2 Colonial America and Ancient Israel   19
3 Nineteenth-Century Zionism : the Christians   25
4 Nineteenth-Century Zionism : the Jews   31
5 Twentieth-Century Zionism : from Basle to Versailles   38
6 Twentieth-Century Zionism : from Jewish Home to
   Jewish Commonwealth   56
7 Twentieth-Century Zionism : from Jewish
   Commonwealth to Jewish State   73

PART TWO   ESSAYS ON THE PRESENT AND THE FUTURE
8 Jewish Lobby, Jewish Vote   95
9 The Economics of Israeli Existence   107
10 Palestinian Terrorism and Israeli Retaliation   117
11 American Jews and Israelis : the Unequal Partners   124
12 The Geopolitics of Population   144
13 Interlocking the United States and Israel   152

Notes   159
Selected Bibliography   166
Index   171

Acknowledgments

Making acknowledgments is perhaps the most pleasant chore a writer has. In the first place, since it is usually the last part of a book to be done, it signifies the end of a long labor. In the second, thanking those who helped bring the labor to its end is both good manners and good therapy.

I am deeply grateful to my wife, Dr Florence Wolfson Glick, who despite her own important work found the time to read critically every word I have written. More than once did she save me and the reader from some stylistic or substantive idiocy. I am also grateful to my graduate assistants, Ellen Bateman and David Jervis, and to my undergraduate assistants, Rena A. Castagnaro, Melus Dey-Nock, Marnina W. Glick, Kenneth O'Hanlon, Carolyn Oscar, Teresa M. Roebuck, and Sheldon Singer.

Some of my colleagues at Temple University were very helpful: the members of the Committee on Research and Study Leaves, for a sabbatical and a monetary grant; Dr Charles A. Joiner, former Chairman of the Department of Political Science; Dr Franklin H. Littell, Professor of Religion; Dr Benjamin Schoenfeld, Professor of Political Science; Dr George W. Wheeler, Dean of the College of Liberal Arts, and George Brightbill, Sandi Thompson, and Barbara Wright, all of the University Library. But since I wrote this book while serving as Coordinator of Political Science at Temple's branch campus in Ambler, Pennsylvania, I am especially grateful for the aid of people there. They are Dr Sidney Halpern, Dean of the Ambler Campus; Dr Richard A. Brashares, Associate Dean; Marilyn E. Froehlich, Assistant Dean for Academic Services; Bonnie Frumer, Assistant Dean for Academic Advising; Dr Lee L. Schreiber, History Department Coordinator; Eleanor L. Smilas, Administrative Assistant to the Dean; Patricia Corcoran, Phyllis McNeill, and Edith Pirée, three most capable faculty secretaries; and Irene T. Lojeski, my faithful manuscript typist.

Then there are others, unconnected with the University, who helped me in important ways that cannot be described: Dr L. G. Eichner, Dr Sidney N. Franklin, Robin Garay, Max W. Gibbs, Dr B. David Grant, Michael Grunberger, the librarian of Philadelphia's unique Gratz College, Pamela Hard, Florence Leffler, and Dr Silas L. Warner. I would also like to thank the Israeli government's Central Bureau of Statistics, the *Jewish Exponent*, the *Jewish Frontier*, the Jewish Publication Society of America, the *New York Times*, and Stackpole Books for permission to use material from their pages.

A number of individuals – in both America and Israel – were kind enough to let me interview them. They are (with the positions and affiliations they had when we talked) the late Yigal Allon, Foreign Minister; Yosef Almogi, Minister of Labor; Shulamit Aloni, member of the Israeli parliament; Mordechai M. Bar-On, head of the youth department of the World Zionist Organization; Techiya Bat-Oren, a leading Israeli feminist and secularist; Meir Caiserman, director of an immigrant absorption center near Jerusalem; his wife, Rachel Caiserman, of the Israel Liaison Office of the American Professors for Peace in the Middle East; Geula Cohen, member of the Israeli parliament; Professor Moshe Davis, head of the Institute of Contemporary Jewry at the Hebrew University of Jerusalem; Meir Dayon, Consul for Economic Affairs of the Consulate-General of Israel in Philadelphia; Abba Eban, Foreign Minister; the late Levi Eshkol, Prime Minister; Ori Even-Tov, of Israel Military Industries, on leave as Research Associate of the Foreign Policy Research Institute of Philadelphia; Dr Ze'ev Falk, Professor of Law at the Hebrew University; Betty Freeman, Assistant Executive Director of the Philadelphia office of the State of Israel Bonds Organization; Zvi Gabay, Cultural Attaché of the Consulate-General of Israel in Philadelphia; S. P. Goldberg, Assistant Director Emeritus of the Council of Jewish Federations and Welfare Funds; Rabbi Shlomo Goren, Ashkenazic Chief Rabbi of Israel; Rivka Hadary, Director of the Israel Liaison Office of the American Professors for Peace in the Middle East; Dr Paul L. Hanna, Emeritus Professor of History and Social Sciences at the University of Florida in Gainesville; Dr Yehoshafat Harkabi, Professor of International Relations at the Hebrew University; Avraham Harman, President of the Hebrew University; Dr Edy Kaufman, Lecturer in International Relations and Latin American Affairs at the Hebrew University; Irving Kessler, Executive Vice-Chairman of the United Israel Appeal; Dr Jacob Landau, Professor of Political Science at the Hebrew University; Ezekiel Leikin, Director of the Philadelphia District of the Zionist Organization of America; Dr Solomon L. Levy, Director of Programs of the National Council of Jewish Women; David Mallach, Associate Director for International Concerns of the Jewish Community Relations Council of Greater Philadelphia; Daniel Mann, Executive Director of the Jewish Community Council of Greater Washington; Theodore R. Mann, Chairman of the Conference of Presidents of Major American Jewish Organizations and Chairman of the National Jewish Community Relations Advisory Council; the late Golda Meir, Prime Minister; Dr Noach Milgrom, Professor of Psychology at Tel-Aviv University; Arye Naor, Cabinet Secretary of the government of Israel; Dr Yitzchak E. Nebenzahl, the State Comptroller and Public Complaints Commissioner; Ya'acov Paran, Consul at the Consulate-General of Israel in Philadelphia; Shimon Peres, Leader of the Opposition in the Israeli Parliament; the late Arye Pincus, Chairman of the Jewish Agency and of the World Zionist Organization; Yitzchak Rabin, Israeli Ambassador to the United States; Dr Larry Rubin, Executive Director of the Jewish Community Relations Council of Greater Philadelphia; Lieutenant-Colonel (Reserves) Avraham Schwartz, Israel Defense Forces; Eliezer Whartman, Jerusalem correspondent of the Philadelphia *Jewish Exponent;* Haim J. Zadok, Chairman of the Defense and Foreign ,Affairs Committee of the Israeli Parliament; and Major-General Eliahu Ze'ira, Chief of Israeli Military Intelligence.

Finally, I owe a great deal to Michael Holdsworth, editor, of George Allen & Unwin, who encouraged me to write this book; and my students, who taught me by their questions and comments.

EDWARD BERNARD GLICK
Ambler, Pennsylvania

Where there is much desire to learn, there of necessity will be much arguing, much writing, many opinions; for opinion in good men is but knowledge in the making.

(John Milton, *Areopagitica*, 1644)

The right to change, and complain, and change some more is the definition of hope.

(Flora Lewis, *New York Times*, 1980)

I

Introduction

This is a book about a relationship between two countries and an ethnic group residing within one of them. The relationship has a past, a present, and a future – all connected by cords of history, geography, religion, culture, psychology, and politics.

Why write about it? One reason is that no one else has satisfactorily dealt with the interrelated dynamics of the triangle. Another is that I hold some very strong opinions about the relationship, especially about what is happening now and about what will or should be happening later. I hope to express them without merely rehashing the past, riding the media headlines of the present, or being ridiculously unrealistic about the future.

In Part One a largely historical approach has been adopted until about 1949. I stopped there because that is the year in which Israel was admitted into the United Nations, capping the international community's recognition of the Jewish people's right to a sovereign state of its own. In Part Two a switch is made to a largely topical approach which is occasionally polemical and occasionally autobiographical. Essentially, Part Two is a vehicle for developing the reasoning and logic for my own strongly held views. But when one talks about views, and the facts underpinning them, one inevitably slides into the question of whether there really is such a thing as an uninterpreted fact, uninfluenced by the person experiencing it, observing it, or writing about it.

On 22 September 1979 and again on 15 December 1980 United States orbiting satellites spotted previously undetected and unexplained light flashes off the coast of South Africa. Because there was a possibility that they were due to secret nuclear testing, the American government made available to two panels of atmospheric and nuclear scientists all the data at its command, asking them to study them independently and report their conclusions publicly.

One panel reported that the flashes were indeed evidences of man-made nuclear explosions; the other, that they were evidences of entirely natural phenomena. If this kind of difference of judgment and conclusion occurs in the more exact disciplines of physics and engineering, is it not more likely to happen when the disciplines are the social sciences and the subject has to do with the Arab-Israel problem, none of which is very exact or without controversy?

The Arab-Israel problem – particularly as it relates to the Palestinians, who, I believe, are now a separate national entity – is one of the most emotional and intractable problems in modern political history. This is so because there is right on both sides. Both Israeli Jews and Palestinian Arabs have legitimate claims that are mutually exclusive and not subject to compromise. It was precisely because of this dual legitimacy and mutual exclusivity that the United Nations called for Palestine's partition into Jewish and Arab states in the late 1940s.

As an American scholar dealing with Israel and the Middle East, as well as an American Jew who was born into the Zionist movement, I am well aware of the pitfalls awaiting anyone who writes about the problem. Within the context of my background and belief system, I shall be as objective as humanly possible. Nevertheless, I expect both criticism and controversy – perhaps more from Israelis and my fellow Diaspora Zionists than from Palestinian Arabs and their partisans. This is not because I enjoy criticism and controversy or want to create them for the sake of selling more books. Rather it is because I want to join those who are trying to build a bridge of mutual acceptance that will allow a sovereign Jewish Israel to live in secure peace with the Arabs – who will always be their neighbors and must some day be their friends.

Part One

The Historical Setting

2

Colonial America and Ancient Israel

From reading American newspapers, listening to American radio, and watching American television one might conclude that America's day-and-night preoccupation with things Israeli and Palestinian is of recent vintage. One might even assume, incorrectly, that it is due to the influence of the so-called Jewish lobby, aided in its efforts by the Nazi Holocaust during World War II, the sorry plight of those Jews who managed to survive it after the war, and the turmoil that developed and still continues in the Middle East.

In fact, geography and history tell us otherwise. While the first British settlers in North America never officially called their settlements New Jerusalem, New Zion, or New Israel, as some of them had wished, as their descendants moved the British frontier to the north, south, and west they placed hundreds of biblically derived names on the map of the future United States. Thus, for example, there is a Jericho in Alabama, an Eden in Arizona, a Samaria in Idaho, a Hebron in North Dakota, a Lake Sinai in South Dakota, a Jordan in Illinois, a Zoar in Massachusetts, an Elisha in Rhode Island, a Sodom in Ohio, a Bethlehem in Pennsylvania, a New Canaan in Connecticut, and a Goshen County in Wyoming. Fifteen places in almost as many states are called Zion. Four places in four states are called Jerusalem. And no less than twenty-seven towns, cities, and countries are called Salem. No other country has so symbolically linked its geographic nomenclature with that of the Land of Israel.

There are good historical reasons for this linkage. The Pilgrims were God-fearing readers of the Jewish Old Testament. It is a book they not only believed in and tried to live by; it is also one which not a few of them frequently read and copied in the original Hebrew. We know that in the 1600s William Bradford – a passenger on the *Mayflower*, a leader of the Pilgrims, and the second governor of the Plymouth Colony in Massachusetts – kept an exercise book into which he wrote Hebrew verses from the Old Testament followed by his own translations of them into English. In his *History of the Plimoth Plantation*, which contains samples of his Hebrew handwriting, he wrote : [1]

> Though I am growne aged, yet I have had a longing desire to see with my own eyes, something of that most ancient language, and holy tongue, in which the law and Oracles of God were write[n]; and in which God and angels spake to the holy patriarchs of old time; and what names were given to things from creation. And though I cannot attaine to much herein, yet I am refreshed to have seen some glimpse hereof (as Moyses saw the land of Canan a farr of). My aime and desire is, to see how the words and phrases lye in the holy texte; and to discerne somewhat of the same for my owne contente.

This Christian Pilgrim interest in the Jewish Holy Tongue and Holy Book was shared by other Americans – before, during, and after the Revolutionary War. When Harvard, the first English-speaking university in the New World, was founded in 1636, Hebrew was a required subject. A student who could not translate the Bible from Hebrew into Latin could not hope to become one of its alumni either. A teacher who knew no Hebrew could not hope to teach anything else at King's College, the original name of Columbia University. This was so because its first president, Samuel Johnson, was convinced that Hebrew was absolutely indispensable for a college education. Hebrew became a compulsory component of Yale University's curriculum when the Reverend Ezra Stiles became its president in 1778. For many years Stiles maintained a correspondence with Hebron-born and -ordained Sephardic Jewish scholar Raphael Haim Isaac Carigal. When Carigal was in Barbados in July 1775 he received a letter from Stiles. After recounting the Battle of Bunker Hill to Carigal, Stiles turned to a discussion of Hebrew. He called it 'that most excellent & devine Language' and asked Carigal to write a short letter in Hebrew to his son, so that he might be inspired to study it more attentively. 'For the same purpose', Stiles added, '& to teach & p[er]fect me in the epistolary stile, I should be glad if you would write some of your Letters to me in Hebrew. May I hope for one in Answer to my long Hebrew Letter of 1773.' [2]

A nineteenth-century example of the linkage between Hebrew, Israel, the Old Testament, and American Christianity are Joseph Smith's actions. Smith was the founder of the Mormon Church, perhaps the only Christian denomination truly indigenous to the United States. In the Mormon archives in Salt Lake City there is the following document.[3]

> Mr. Joseph Smith Junr. has attended a full course of Hebrew lessons under my tuition; & has been indefatigable in acquiring the principles of the sacred Language of the Old Testament Scriptures in their original tongue. He has so far accomplished a knowledge of it, that he is able to translate to my entire satisfaction; & by prosecuting the study he will be able to become a [sic] proficient in Hebrew. I take this opportunity of thanking him for his industry, & his marked kindness towards me.
>
> J. Seixas
>
> Kirtland Ohio March 30th 1836

As for the early twentieth century, there is a letter, dated 20 October 1902, from Secretary of State John Hay to the Reverend Marcus H. Dubov of Evansville, Indiana. It concerns the secretary's appreciated efforts on behalf of persecuted Jews in Romania and reads as follows.[4]

> I received your letter, man of God, and I was happy that my efforts on behalf of your persecuted brethren in the kingdom of Roumania pleased you. Peace to you and your congregation Bnai Moshe.
>
> I ask from the Lord our God that He bless the people of your covenant in Evansville, in all you do, both in word and deed. May the God of peace be with you forever. I am he who loves you.

This letter is remarkable because, except for the words 'Department of State' and 'Washington', as well as the date, Dubov's name, his address on the top of the letter, and Hay's signature on the bottom – all in English – the rest of it is written by the secretary's own hand in beautiful and idiomatically correct modern Hebrew.

Finally, Edmund Wilson, one of the finest American social and literary critics of this century, has described how he discovered Hebrew.[5]

I had always had a certain curiosity about Hebrew, and I was piqued a little at the thought that my grandfather could read something that I couldn't, so, finding myself one autumn in Princeton, with the prospect of spending the winter, I enrolled in a Hebrew course at the Theological Seminary from which my grandfather [a Presbyterian minister] had graduated in 1846. I have thus acquired a smattering that has enabled me to work through Genesis . . . and this first acquaintance with the Hebrew text has . . . been to me a revelation. In the first place, the study of a Semitic language gives one insights into a whole point of view, a system of mental habits, that differs radically from those of the West.

Now, one should not push the Hebrew–Old Testament–United States–modern Israel connection too far. After all, of America's approximately 3,000 secular colleges and universities, only three – Columbia, Dartmouth, and Yale – have Hebrew in their official seals. One does not have to know Hebrew to get into or out of Harvard today. One does not have to know Hebrew to teach another subject at Columbia. One does not have to know Hebrew to be the current president of Yale. And one certainly does not have to know it as a prerequisite for becoming the American Secretary of State.

But one should not dismiss entirely the importance of Hebrew in the connection either. It would of course be foolish to argue that the United States has supported the restoration of Jewish sovereignty because many of its more educated Christian citizens knew Hebrew several centuries ago or because a tiny fraction of them know it today. However, it would be equally foolish not to recognize that the Hebrew/Old Testament element in America's intellectual history nourished the soil in which America's support for the modern Jewish state sprouted, especially among Christians.

Many American Christian clergymen today are spellbinding preachers who sprinkle their sermons with Old Testament images and metaphors. The same was true for their colleagues of the revolutionary period. The colonial condition vis-a-vis Great Britain was likened to that of the Israelite slaves in ancient Egypt. The colonial struggle against the British Crown was compared to that of Moses against Pharaoh. When the Founding Fathers were discussing the Seal of the United States, Thomas Jefferson, Benjamin Franklin, and John Adams submitted a design depicting the

Israelites crossing the Red Sea – with Moses standing on one side
of the parted waters and Pharaoh pursuing him on the other side.
In his *The Separation of the Jewish Tribes, After the Death of
Solomon, Accounted for, and Applied to the Present Day . . .*[6]
William Gordon argued, on 4 July 1777, that just as the ten
Hebrew tribes were driven to rebellion by the tyranny of Solomon's
son, King Rehoboam, so were the thirteen British colonies driven
to the same action by the tyranny of their sovereign, King George
III. True, this separation of the tribes weakened and ultimately
destroyed Hebrew government in the area. But, according to
Gordon, this was because the unwise Hebrews had replaced one
monarchy with another, whereas the wise Americans had replaced
their monarchy with a republic.

In 1775 Samuel Langdon had written : 'The Jewish Government,
according to the original constitution which was divinely inspired,
if considered merely in a civil view, was a perfect republic . . . The
civil polity of Israel is doubtless an excellent model . . .'[7] Thirteen
years later, in his sermon entitled *The Republic of the Israelites an
Example to the American States*, he declared that the ancient Jews
'may be considered as a pattern to the world in all ages, and from
them we will learn what will exalt our character, and what will
depress and bring us to ruin'. In this same sermon Langdon, like
William Gordon, expressed the belief that the early Israelites had
lost their statehood because they had abandoned their original
governing system of cooperating tribes. In their own ways both
men were making a case for what the modern world calls federalism,
a means of governance which they traced back to the tribes of
Israel.

A third sermon of the period was by Abiel Abbot. Entitled *Traits
of Resemblance in the People of the United States of America to
Ancient Israel*, it was delivered in 1799. Abbot argued that no
country in the late eighteenth century was so much like ancient
Israel as was the United States. The two resembled each other in
their happiness, in their distinctiveness from other nations, and in
their having been favored with divine presence, divine providence,
and divine protection from their enemies. For these reasons Abbot
counseled his countrymen to think of the new American nation as
a New Zion and to conduct their lives in accordance with the
principles of the Gospels.

Finally, there is the linkage between America and the Lost Ten
Tribes of Israel. The last verse of Isaiah 18 reads :

At that time tribute shall be brought to the Lord of Hosts from a people tall and smooth-skinned, dreaded near and far, a nation strong and proud, whose land is scoured by rivers. They shall bring it to Mount Zion, the place where men invoke the name of the Lord of Hosts.

To Ethan Smith the land that Isaiah is referring to is America and the people that he is referring to are the American Indians. Smith somehow managed to spin a web that enmeshed the Ten Tribes, the American Indians, the United States, the Jews' dispersion, their predestined return to Zion, and the Prophet Isaiah. He did this, in 1823, in his *View of the Hebrews: Exhibiting the Destruction of Jerusalem, the Certain Restoration of Judah and Israel, the Present State of Judah and Israel, and an Address of the Prophet Isaiah Relative to their Restoration.*[8] Smith's research led him to the conclusion that the American Indians are the descendants of the original Ten Tribes. With the help of the United States, they and all contemporary children of Israel will be saved and returned to the Holy Land.

There is an important difference between Smith's work and that of Abbot, Gordon, and Langdon. While all four of them related Judeo-Christian history and theology to the American condition, Smith added a political dimension. He advocated the bodily return of the Jewish people, presumably in full sovereignty, to the actual geographical area of the Middle East in which they commenced their history some five millennia ago.

3

Nineteenth-Century Zionism: the Christians

Americans did not begin to feel secure about their own political independence until the first quarter of the nineteenth century. They were not entirely sure about it until after the war of 1812 with Great Britain and the proclamation of the Monroe Doctrine in 1823, which happened to be the year in which Ethan Smith wrote his book supporting Jewish restoration in Palestine. As well as Smith there were quite a few American Christians who espoused this idea.

In 1807 the *Christian Observer* predicted that a significant rise in the flow of Jews to Palestine – there had always been a trickle – would begin in 1866. It was off the mark by only some fifteen years, which saw the beginning of what in Zionist history is reverently known as *ha-aliyah harishonah* (the First Immigration). In 1816 the *Weekly Register*, musing over the plight of Europe's Jews after Napoleon's defeat, wondered why wealthy Jews did not exploit the weakness of the Turkish Empire and buy Palestine. In 1818 Thomas Kennedy, a Catholic who reportedly had never seen a Jew in person, spoke Zionist words during a presentation in favor of equality for the Jews of Maryland :[1]

> But if we are christians in deed and in truth, we must believe that the Jewish nation will again be restored to the favour and protection of God . . . And he who led their fathers through the deserts, has promised to lead them again to their native land. He who raised up and called Cyrus by name, can . . . raise up a deliverer to his once favored nation; and it is probable that the time is not far distant when this great event shall take place . . . [May] we not hope that the banners of the children of Israel shall again be unfurled on the walls of Jerusalem on the Holy Hill of Zion?

The first American President (although he was not in office at the time) to endorse Jewish return was John Adams. In 1819 he responded to a letter from a Jewish citizen, in which he said:[2]

If I could let my imagination loose . . . I could find it in my heart to wish that you had been at the head of a hundred thousand Israelites . . . marching with them into Judea & making a conquest of that country & restoring your nation to the dominion of it. For I really wish the Jews again in Judea an independent nation. For I believe [that] . . . once restored to an independent government & no longer persecuted they would soon wear away some of the asperities and peculiarities of their character & possibly in time become liberal Unitarian christians for your Jehovah is our Jehovah & your God . . . is our God.

It has already been noted that Joseph Smith, the founder of Mormonism, studied Hebrew in the 1830s. In 1842 Orson Hyde, his fellow Hebrew student and now an elder in the church, published his *A Voice from Jerusalem*, which sketched his travels and ministry to Germany, Turkey, and Palestine. On the Mount of Olives Hyde enacted the first formal resolution of the church. It took the form of a prayer, later included in the Mormon prayer book, for the restoration of the Holy Land and its holy capital city to the Jews. On the trip Hyde also sent a letter home in which he wrote: 'The fact is, this land belongs to the Jews; and the present formation thereof shows to me that it is fast working back into the hands of its rightful heirs.'[3] (In October 1979 a delegation of 2,000 Mormons, led by the president of the church, contributed $1 million and dedicated the Orson Hyde Memorial Park on the western slopes of the Mount of Olives.)

Three years later, after Smith's murder at the hands of a mob, his successor, Brigham Young, together with the other members of the Mormon Council of Twelve, addressed a proclamation to the leaders of the temporal world. In it was the following passage: 'And we further testify that the Jews among all nations are hereby commanded, in the name of the Messiah, to prepare to return to Jerusalem in Palestine . . . and also to organize and establish their own political government.'[4] When four leading Mormons left for a tour of Palestine in October 1872 Young penned this benediction for them:[5]

When you go to the Land of Palestine, we wish you to dedicate and consecrate that Land to the Lord, that it may be blessed with fruitfulness, preparatory to the return of the Jews in fulfillment of prophecy, and the accomplishment of the purposes of our Heavenly Father.

To be sure, Smith, like former President John Adams before him and other gentiles after him, were grinding a Christological axe on a Judaic stone. They saw the Jews' return to Palestine as a theological precondition for the latter's conversion to Christianity and for the second coming of Christ. Nevertheless, these constant connections between modern Palestine and modern Jewry, regardless of motive, helped to develop the psychological set for later Christian acceptance of the modern State of Israel.

An early Zionist zealot of the period was the son of one of Philadelphia's oldest Quaker families. He came to Jerusalem in 1844 as the Christian Warder Cresson and died there as the Jew Michael Boaz Israel. His abiding interest was in the return not of Jesus Christ to earth but of the Jews to Palestine. For this and especially his conversion to Judaism, he was declared legally insane when he went back to settle his affairs in Philadelphia, a town founded on religious tolerance and still called the City of Brotherly Love.

The insanity decision was reversed just before Cresson published, in 1852, his polemic, *The Key of David: David the True Messiah, Or the Annointed of the God of Jacob*. In this and other writings he maintained, as did later Jewish thinkers, that a lasting Jewish presence in Palestine must rest on a sound agricultural base. He actually envisaged some of the current forms of the Israeli collectives, the *kibbutz* and the *moshav*. In the 1854 issue of the Philadelphia Jewish magazine *The Occident* he wrote:

It is therefore proposed that the means be provided to begin a settlement or agricultural colony in Palestine; and in order to prevent a monopoly of power or of wealth by any one person, let the settlement be divided into small families . . . united to each other for protection and defence, when required.

Cresson foresaw two other problems of modern Zionism and modern Israel in his article in *The Occident*. One was the objection of ultra-Orthodox Jews to the creation of a Jewish state without the express intervention of the Messiah. The other was Israel's need for an American security guarantee. On the first point he wrote that 'it surely must be right for us to endeavor to promote the happy future by some exertions of our own', a kind of God-helps-those-who-help-themselves attitude. On the second point he wrote : 'We would most respectfully solicit the protection of the President and government of the United States of America, especially during our infancy.'

In 1882, a year of terrible pogroms in the Russian Pale, Congressman Samuel Cox wrote this passage about the Jewish link to Jerusalem :[6]

[In] the full blaze of history, one cannot help but feel that this is especially the city of the Jews. Christians may fight for and hold its holy places; Moslems may guard from all other eyes the tombs of David and Solomon· the site of the temple on Mount Moriah may be decorated by the mosques of Omar and Aksa; but if ever there was a material object on earth closely allied with a people, it is this city of Jerusalem with the Jews. In all their desolation and wandering, was there ever a race so sensitive as to the city of its heart and devotion? All the resources . . . of this rare race . . . have been called in to summarize . . . the soreness of its weeping and the tearfulness of its anguish over the fate of Jerusalem and the restlessness of its exiles.

William E. Blackstone enters the picture now. On 5 March 1891 he sent to President Benjamin Harrison, a 'memorial' – actually a petition – entitled 'Palestine for the Jews', signed by over 400 prominent people.[7] If the great powers, he asked, could, in the Berlin Treaty of 1878, give Bulgaria to the Bulgarians and Serbia to the Serbians, why could they not give Palestine to the Jews? 'Does not Palestine as rightfully belong to the Jews?'

What makes Blackstone's words memorable is not only what he said but the manner in which he said them and the manner in which he arranged to let both the politicians and the public know about them. Five years before Theodor Herzl published his *Der Judenstaat* (*The Jewish State*) and six years before Herzl convened the first World Zionist Congress, we find a gentile transforming what had before been largely religious and emotional yearnings of Jews for Palestine into a modern political manifestation of Jewish nationalism in Palestine. And he did it very deftly.

On the external level Blackstone asked the President and his Secretary of State, James G. Blaine, to use their good offices with the rulers of Russia, Great Britain, Germany, Austria-Hungary, Turkey, Italy, Spain, France, Belgium, Holland, Denmark, Portugal, Romania, Serbia, Bulgaria, and Greece to support a Jewish-run Palestine. His argument was that 'all the European nations sympathizing with the sad condition of the Jews in Russia, and not yet wishing them to be crowded into their own countries, will . . . cheerfully assent to this restoration to Palestine as the most natural alternative'.

Domestically, Blackstone tried to make the President aware that the petition was not the outgrowth of a group of nobodies but of a national conference of very notable Christians and Jews, the first such meeting ever held in the United States. The petition was signed by people from Chicago, Boston, New York, Philadelphia, Baltimore, and Washington. Of the 400 signatories at least 175 were Christians. If these Christians did not represent all the major geographical regions of America, they were at least a good cross-section of the movers and shakers of the Northeast and the Middle West. Given the subject of Blackstone's memorial to President Harrison, this was no small accomplishment.

The university world was represented by faculty members of Columbia, the provost of the University of Pennsylvania, the presidents of Beloit College and Wheaton College, the former president of American-supported Robert College in Turkey, as well as teachers from the Chicago, Andover, and Union Theological Seminaries.

The judicial and political worlds were represented by the Chief Justice of the United States Supreme Court, a member of the Illinois Supreme Court, the president of the Board of Commissioners of the District of Columbia (which is the official name of the city of Washington), the mayors of Baltimore, New York, Philadelphia, and Chicago, the Speaker of the House of Representatives, the chairman of the House Foreign Affairs Committee, and ten other members of Congress, including William McKinley, who later became President of the United States.

Religion was represented by such people as the Catholic archbishops of both Chicago and Baltimore, the secretary of the American Baptist Missionary Union, the corresponding secretary of the American Bible Society, the general secretary of the Evangelical Alliance of the United States, the secretary of the Board of Home

Missions of the Presbyterians, and the bishop of the Methodist Episcopal Church in New York. The media were represented by publishers and editors from, among others, *Harper's Weekly*, the *Chicago Tribune*, the *Chicago Daily News*, the *Boston Daily Globe*, the *Boston Herald*, the *New York Times*, the *Philadelphia Enquirer*, the *Philadelphia Bulletin*, the *Baltimore American*, and the *Baltimore Daily News*. As for the worlds of business and finance, such people as James C. Fargo, Charles Scribner, Russell Sage, John D. Rockefeller, William Rockefeller, Cyrus W. Field, Chauncey M. Depew, William E. Dodge, Cyrus H. McCormick, and J. Pierpont Morgan signed Blackstone's pro-Jewish Palestine petition.

Blackstone sent his petition to the President with a letter of transmittal. The letter's very first paragraph included this phrase : 'the undersigned begs to state that he has not sought for a multitude of signatures, but only representative names, and the cordial endorsement which the Memorial has received, gives assurance that the signatures could be indefinitely multiplied'. Neither Blackstone nor Harrison could be sure about this; Blackstone could hardly prove that it was true and Harrison could hardly prove that it was not. The important fact is that, in convening the meeting of Christians and Jews, having them sign a statement on behalf of a Zionist solution to the problems of Czarist Russian Jewry, and presenting the statement to the President, Blackstone was using what the political scientists of America call 'interest group articulation' and what the plain folks know as old-fashioned lobbying and pressure group politics. It is one of America's oldest democratic traditions – and it often works.

4

Nineteenth-Century Zionism: The Jews

There used to be a beautiful marriage custom in some of the ghettos of medieval Europe. Before the wedding day the guests would receive an invitation that read somewhat as follows :

> The parents of the groom and the parents of the bride would be honored if you would share with them the joy and blessing of witnessing the marriage of their son and daughter. With God's help, the wedding will take place on such and such a date at such and such an hour in the courtyard of the restored Holy Temple in the Holy City of Jerusalem. But if, in his wisdom and mystery, the Holy One, praised be His Name, should still wish the Messiah to tarry, then the wedding will take place instead at our local synagogue at the same hour and on the same day.

Pious Jews do not play this precious piece of 'Let's pretend' anymore. But thrice daily they ask God : 'Return in mercy to Your city of Jerusalem and dwell in it as You have promised.' Even not so pious Jews, in those countries where they have been allowed to worship freely, end their fast and prayers on Yom Kippur with the long sound of the ram's horn and the short cry of 'Next year in Jerusalem'.

How did the Jews of nineteenth-century America fit into this scheme of thinking, this pattern of behavior? When the observant among them prayed for Jerusalem three times a day, were they praying for a literal return? When they and their less observant, but still identifying, brethren (some of whom came to the synagogue only three times a year) proclaimed 'Next year in Jerusalem' did they really mean it? Or did they recite it merely as the last ritual of their most holy Day of Atonement before, fatigued and famished, they rushed home to break the fast? And if they meant it, how did they mean it? Was Jerusalem (and Zion, and Israel, and Palestine) just an ancient, still-standing place whose name they regularly invoked out of habit, tradition, custom, even fear? Or was it a place to be restored, together with the land around it, to Jewish political control? If it was the latter, was it for themselves as well, or only for other Jews – for their unfortunate coreligionists in countries like anti-Semitic Germany, Italy, Poland, Romania, and Czarist Russia? Or, indeed, did most American Jews of the period agree with Rabbi David Phillipson's famous remark of 1895, 'The United States is our Palestine and Washington our Jerusalem'.[1]

The fact is that during most of the century specific activity by American Jews to restore Palestine was meager and sporadic. During all of the century the actual number of American Jewish proponents of the idea was small by any measure.

We saw in Chapter 3 that President John Adams, in his reply to a letter written in 1819, supported Jewish statehood in Palestine, or Judea, as he called it. The man to whom he was replying was Mordecai Manuel Noah, an American Jewish journalist, dramatist, lawyer, and one-time consul in Tunis. As a result of his stay in the Middle East and a visit to Europe, Noah came to take positions and actions that foreshadowed later political Zionism. In 1818 he said: 'When the signal for breaking the Turkish Sceptre in Europe is given, the Jews . . . will possess themselves once more of Syria and take rank among the nations of the world.'[2] Noah's reference to Syria rather than to Palestine is another proof that the name 'Palestine' did not really enter the geopolitical lexicon until much later – not in fact until the Balfour Declaration of 1917 and the incorporation of the Declaration into the League of Nations Palestine Mandate in 1922. That is why there were Syrians in Mordecai Manuel Noah's time, as there are Syrians in modern times, who regarded and who regard *all* of what are today Israel, Jordan, the West Bank, and the Gaza Strip as part of Greater, or Southern, Syria.

In 1824 Noah said: 'We will return to Zion as we went forth, bringing back the faith we carried away with us.' In 1825 he persuaded a Christian friend to buy a piece of land on Grand Island in the Niagara River near Buffalo, New York. Called Ararat, it was conceived as a temporary substitute, a way-station, in the New

World for the Jewish Palestinian homeland in the Old World of the Middle East. Here again, Noah demonstrated a certain ability to predict the future accurately. For while his Ararat scheme was scrapped because of insufficient response, in its conception it was very much like more successful schemes later. For example, in the late 1930s and early 1940s at least two Socialist-Zionist organizations, Habonim (The Builders) and Hashomer Hatza-ir (The Young Guard), set up training farms in southern New Jersey modeled on the *kibbutz*. From them young Americans were sent out to settle on existing *kibbutzim* or to start new ones in Palestine.

Noah was also one of the first American Jews who realized decades before the organization and efforts of the so-called Jewish lobby that Zionist goals in Palestine would not be achieved without the help of Christians in America. And so he made it his habit to address them frequently, especially the restorationist evangelicals. But whenever he addressed the latter he asked them to stop trying to convert the Jews to Christianity and to rely instead 'on the fulfillment of the prophecies and the will of God for obtaining the objects they have in view after the great event shall have arrived'. He implored all denominations of Christians to understand that, no matter whether they had in mind the pre-Jesus prophecies of the Old Testament or the post-Jesus prophecies of the New Testament, both sets of prophecies 'relate to the literal and not [just] to the spiritual restoration of the Jews'.

But he always stressed that the Jews needed the support of the Christians. Speaking to a group of them at the Tabernacle in New York City, he said:

But we cannot move alone . . . The power and influence of our Christian brethren . . . must be invoked . . . You believe in the second coming of Jesus of Nazareth. That second advent, Christians, depends upon you. It cannot come to pass, by your own admission, until the Jews are restored.

And when Noah spoke of Christians he specifically meant American Christians:

Let me . . . impress upon your minds the most important fact, that the liberty and independence of the Jewish nation may grow out of a single effort which this country may make in their behalf. That effort is to secure for them a permission to purchase and hold land in security and peace; their titles and possessions confirmed; their fields and flocks undisturbed.

While Mordecai Manuel Noah was a significant member of that small and early band of pre-Herzl Jewish Zionists in the United States, he was not the only one. Another was Rabbi Isaac Leeser of Philadelphia. It was Leeser who started the Jewish monthly *The Occident*, which opened its pages to the Christian-turned-Jewish Zionist, Warder Cresson. In the April 1864 issue Leeser published an editorial called 'The future of Palestine'. He employed some of the same arguments for Jewish sovereignty that post-Herzl Zionists were to use thirty-five years later and that Israel and its overseas supporters use today. It is quoted at length because Leeser was the most important Jewish leader in the period before the American Civil War, and because, unlike most other American Jews of German origin, he was as ardently in favor of Zionism as they were apoplectically against it.

Why, Lesser wrote,

should every religion have a home where it is triumphant, and Judaism always have to receive the law from a dominant system. Without a home, ours by right, this must always be . . . and until this once blessed land is blessed again with fertility and a teeming population, will the life struggle of Israel continue . . . The desert would soon be made to blossom as the rose; streams would flow through now barren soil; waste cities would be rebuilt . . . [Those] who fancy the thing a ridiculous notion . . . may find it to their interest to labor for the restoration of Palestine . . . a spot where the ark of our covenant may rest without being exposed to the malevolence of dissentient neighbors, and the ill-usage which we have hitherto always encountered, and shall probably hereafter meet in all lands where we are strangers, whether these be ruled by Nazarenes [Christians], Mahomedans [Muslims] or Brahmins [Hindus] whether autocratic or republican, whether we are excluded from equal rights or endowed with all the privileges of citizenship. We must ever be in the minority; and . . . we shall always have to complain of slights and insults, of being overlooked . . . of being scorned . . . and denounced . . .

But once again blessed with a government of our own,

though only a small portion of Israelites shall be found in their own land, while the many would prefer to remain in the countries where they now sojourn, and the advantages of which they might not wish to give up, the feelings of the world would necessarily undergo a great change, and the treatment meted out to us would not be what it is now.

If we had our agriculturists, our statesmen, our public teachers, equal to the best found anywhere, who would dare to insult us by stating that 'he knows us only as peddlers, bankers, and merchants', and class us as a whole among smugglers, petty traders and men of low pursuits?

Leeser was obviously acknowledging the existence of American anti-Semitism. He was also predicting that, despite it, American Jews would by and large not immigrate to a Jewish Palestine, as indeed they have not. But anti-Semitism and immigation aside, Leeser, decades before the actual establishment of the modern Israeli state, clearly understood what Zionism and Israel are really all about. He clearly understood that, stripped to the very nakedness of meaning, Israel is simply the only independent state in the world where the majority of the citizens are, and must continue to be, Jews. Otherwise there is no justification for a Jewish state. And Zionism is simply the ideology that postulates the historical, religious, psychological, sociological, and political reasons why that sovereign Jewish majority must reside in at least a portion of the Biblical Land of Israel and in no other place on earth.

Now, one point must be clearly made when one talks about Zionism among nineteenth-century American Jews. For every Mordecai Manuel Noah, for every Rabbi Isaac Leeser, there were thousands and thousands of American Jews who ignored it altogether, and dozens – perhaps hundreds – who opposed it with articulate passion.

A generalized profile of the latter shows them to be mostly of German ancestry, highly assimilated, fairly well-off, religiously affiliated (if at all) with Reform Judaism, and pathologically fearful of stirring up any anti-Semitism and charges of dual loyalty and un-Americanism. Their relationship to Reform Judaism made it easy for them to be anti-Zionist, since the Reform rabbinate was anti-Zionist almost to the eve of Israel's creation in 1948. And the latter's opposition stemmed directly from its theological rejection of the notion that the Jews were a people with a Messianic mission, or even an ethnic group, as Americans know and use the term. Instead, they were simply Americans of the Mosaic faith, just as other citizens were Americans of the Christian faith.

Another reason for Jewish anti-Zionism can be derived from those American Jews who were Zionists. Despite the fact that the acknowledged founder of modern political Zionism, Dr Theodor Herzl, was himself a Germanized Hungarian who was highly assimilated into Western secular culture, most Jews attracted to Zionism were in or from Eastern Europe. These 'unwashed', unassimilated, Yiddish-speaking, often religiously Orthodox, *Ostjuden* were the very types – or stereotypes – that many nineteenth-century American Jews were trying so hard to separate themselves from, especially on a psychological level.

One of the more passionate anti-Zionists of the period was Rabbi Emil G. Hirsch of Chicago. The vehicle that he often used for his polemics was the *Reform Advocate*, the official organ of American Reform Judaism. When William Blackstone organized the first Christian–Jewish dialogue and then sent his 'Palestine for the Jews' petition to President Harrison, Rabbi Hirsch was quite disturbed. Although he admitted that Blackstone's love for the Jews was 'genuine', he called his dream of Jewish nationality and Jewish restoration 'a fool's errand'. 'We modern Jews', he wrote, 'do not wish to be restored to Palestine . . . We will not go back . . . to form a nationality of our own.' [3]

Hirsch was particularly perturbed at the petition to the President: 'We are sorry that such a memorial ever was composed and laid before the Executive head of our government . . .' And as for its signatories – both Christian and Jewish – he wrote :

> It is certainly a remarkable company of names which grace the paper . . . [and] hurry to show their sympathy with the unfortunate Jews of Russia. The tribute of gratitude should not be stinted to the gentlemen who did not refuse to plead the cause of unfortunate men and women, though not of their own faith. That so many Jewish signatures should have been gotten to the petition is . . . less gratifying to us.

But Blackstone already knew and anticipated the negative reactions of American Reform rabbis. For in the letter that accompanied his petition to President Harrison he included this paragraph :

[While] a very few, of what are termed ultra-radical, reformed, Jewish Rabbis have renounced their belief in ancient Scriptures, and openly proclaim that the Jews should amalgamate with the various nations, wherein they are scattered, the great body of the Jews, both clergy and laity, still cling to their time honored hopes of national restoration and will quickly respond to any such opportunity with abundant energy, means, and enthusiasm.

How quickly, how energetically, how enthusiastically, with what means, and in what numbers American Jews responded to Zionism becomes especially relevant as we reach Zionism's watershed : the successful convening of the first World Zionist Congress in Switzerland three years before the end of the nineteenth century.

5

Twentieth-Century Zionism: from Basle to Versailles

The Romans sacked the Second Temple in the year 70 of the Common Era. For centuries after that there were people – I have mentioned only the Americans among them – who prophesied, prayed, preached, planned, proposed, pronounced, proclaimed, and plotted on behalf of the notion that the Jews belong in Palestine and that Palestine should belong to the Jews – again.

One of them was Theodor Herzl. He stands above all the rest as *the* founder of modern political Zionism. Why? For one thing, he wrote *The Jewish State*, which he published at a historically receptive moment, in 1896. For another, his was the guiding hand behind the convening in 1897 of the first World Zionist Congress in the Swiss city of Basle.

Before Herzl Zionism was simply a longing, a philosophy, a religious expression. After him – and he died only seven years after the Basle Congress – Zionism became an entity, a movement, an international organization. It was this organization, helped along by violent anti-Semitism in Eastern Europe and verbal, but still vicious, anti-Semitism in Western Europe, that finally forced its dreams and demands upon the political consciousness of the nations of the world.

The United States is, of course, one of the world's nations. With its annexation of the Hawaiian Islands and, later, the conquest of Puerto Rico and the Philippines from Spain, America had acquired outposts away from its shores. When Herzl entered the arena of history, America was thus well on its way towards becoming a great power, with all the interests and influences that great powers, by definition and deference, possess. How, then, did America and Americans respond to the Herzlian idea of a Jewish state in the middle of the Middle East? How did they especially respond to a world organization that had formally proclaimed that 'Zionism seeks a publicly recognized, legally secured home . . . in Palestine for the Jewish people'?[1]

The immediate reaction among Jews was not very favorable. In the Anglo-Jewish press, that is, English language publications expressly directed to the Jewish community, there were the following reactions. The *Chicago Israelite*, speaking of Herzl and his colleague Max Nordau, and using them to snipe at the non-Reform Jew, said:[2]

A couple of Agnostics like Herzl and Nordau as the Messiah and Elijah of the return is a pretty good joke, but not half so good as the spectacle of a crowd of followers composed of ritualistic Jews, who have staked their whole existence on the letter of the [Jewish religious] law and on traditional Judaism.

The *American Hebrew* said that 'the entire Jewish press of the world with less than half a dozen exceptions has been opposed to the [Zionist] Congress'.[3] The *American Israelite* urged that Zionism be limited to the Czar's stepchildren, unwanted Jews of Eastern Europe. The *Jewish Chronicle* saw 'no good thing' in Zionism. It said that Herzl simplistically viewed 'all Israel's wrongs redressed by the Constitution of a little State in Palestine somewhat weaker than Greece and somewhat stronger than Monaco'. The *Menorah Monthly* ridiculed the Basle Zionist program for its failure to appreciate that Palestine was as sacred to Muslims and Christians as it was to the Jews. The *Jewish Messenger* hoped that Herzl would somehow come to his senses and realize that 'Zionism is not Judaism'. In short, the majority of the English language Jewish press in America, in the words of Milton Plesur, regarded Zionism 'as a temporary aberration in the American-Jewish mentality'.

Interestingly, many of the Christian-sponsored periodicals were less negative; some were quite positive. The *Christian Advocate* claimed that Jews much preferred to live among gentiles. *Christian Work* considered Zionism a 'small affair'. The *Presbyterian Banner* felt that to 'place the oppressed Jews in an impoverished land with "inhumane" Turks would be a [presumably unattainable or unfortunate] dream'. (However, it did not urge that these oppressed Jews be admitted to America.) On the other hand, the *Churchman* wrote that the 'fulfillment of prophecies looking for a final repossession of Palestine by the Old Testament race has never ceased to be thought of and hoped for by Jews and Christians alike'. As for examples of pro-Zionism from members of the Christian clergy, we can cite two : the Reverend I. M. Haldeman and Francis J. Clay Moran, DD. In a sermon mixing politics and piety (as reported in the *New York Times* of 16 December 1901), Haldeman said that the Jews could gain control of Palestine with proper military leadership. Such control would not only be a welcome barrier to Russian imperial encroachment in the Middle East, but also hasten Christ's coming back to earth again. On 30 August 1903 Dr Moran announced in a letter to the *Times* that he was a Christian Zionist. The Zionists, he wrote, were simply trying to carry out the already prophesied plan of the Divine Ruler, which they would do through a republican form of government. In a later letter, published on 21 September 1903, he wrote :

> I wish some one would arise with the voice, the energy, and the enthusiasm of Peter the Hermit, either Christian or Jew, and preach a new crusade for the restoration of the land Jehovah loves to the custody of his people – a crusade not by force of arms, but a moral pressure upon the peoples of the world . . . [to] by peaceful means restore Israel once more to Zion.

What about the secular American press? *Harper's Weekly* asserted that many Christian missionaries viewed Zionism's possible success as a development that might weaken Judaism and make their task of converting Jews easier. The *New York Sun* doubted that Herzl's ideas would have any serious impact on America's Jews. The *Rochester Post Express* acknowledged the emotional pull of Herzl's ideas but thought they would never get much practical support. The *New York Observer* could not see how any scheme that might make Jerusalem into a modern-day Biblical 'market place' could be good or moral. The *New York Post* remarked that Zionism was merely a plan for moving poor Jews to Palestine. Rich Jews, it said, would never take the financial and other risks involved. And the *Boston Transcript* predicted outright failure if implementation of the Zionist program were ever actually to be attempted.

When one considers the response of the secular American press to political Zionism one has to pay special attention to the *New York Times*. First, it was and is the country's most prestigious paper. It really does come closest to being America's newspaper of record. Secondly, this very preeminence is responsible for the dilemma which the *Times* had to face for many years in its handling of Zionism. On the one hand, its famous masthead motto 'All the News That's Fit to Print' forced it to report the Zionist story as it developed. On the other hand, since 1896 – the same year of *Der Judenstaat*'s appearance – the paper has been owned by a highly assimilated, highly 'Americanized', Jewish family of German descent. By marriage and temperament the family was closely linked to the most anti-Zionist elements within American Jewry, especially within the Reform movement. As a result, the owners of the *Times* said and did anti-Zionist things, which was their personal right. But they sometimes allowed their personal right to overwhelm their publishers' duty. As publishers they were perfectly entitled to pursue an anti-Zionist policy on their editorial pages, which they did long after many other American Jews had dropped their anti-Zionism. But they also had the duty to keep these views from straying on to the noneditorial pages. By 1948 the *Times* finally learned how to put the straight news about Israel on its regular pages and its own (by then not always negative) editorial views about Israel on the editorial pages. But for the fifty years that preceded the establishment of the state, this was a journalistic feat that the owners and publishers of the *New York Times* generally could not, would not, and, in fact, did not accomplish.

Thus, on 5 September 1897, ignoring the fact that America had purchased the Louisiana Territory from France, Florida from Spain, and Alaska from Russia, the *Times* referred to Theodor Herzl's plan to try to buy Palestine from the Turks as something having 'the flavor of the Stock Exchange'. On 11 August 1897 it wrote :

Dr Theodor Herzl, originator of the Zionistic scheme that has been so coldly received by those [to] whose attention it has been called in this country . . . is regarded . . . of enough importance to make it worthwhile to print his views frequently in the Austrian papers and those in other parts of Europe.

The inference is grudgingly clear : Zionism might have some relevance for the unfortunate Jews of Europe, but not for the emancipated Jews of America.

The *Times*'s specific response to Herzl's book came on 15 August

1897 : 'The religious world has [noticed] . . . a plan for the re-establishment of Palestine as a Jewish state . . . Dr Herzl says that anti-Semitism is economic and social, not religious.' But to Herzl's argument that the cure for anti-Semitism can only be a sovereign Jewish state, the *Times* answered : 'Both in Europe and America there are many Jews who oppose the founding of a Jewish state on the ground that it could be only a small, weak state, existing by sufferance.' Echoing a tenet of Reform Judaism, the newspaper added : 'It is also urged that Israel's mission is no longer political but purely and simply religious, and that the establishment of the state would do incalculable harm, and could do no good.'

A prominent American Jew who shared this view was Rabbi Isaac Mayer Wise of Cincinnati, the founding father of American Reform Judaism. He was the first president of its seminary, the Hebrew Union College. And his daughter had married Adolph Ochs, the founding father of the family that owns the *New York Times*. In a signed article headlined 'A Jewish State Impossible', which appeared in the *Times* on 10 September 1897, Wise wrote :

The various attempts [in the past] . . . to restore the Judaic nationality proved so many failures. It is therefore self-evident that the Judaic nation, and Judaic nationality as well, are, and have been, extinct these one thousand eight hundred years . . . There never has been an earnest will manifested in the people to return to Palestine and establish a government of their own, although they repeated this wish in their established prayers day after day.

Wise called the Zionist Congress at Basle a meeting of 'Russian emigrants . . . with a few 'Lovers of Zion' from Germany and Austria thrown in. He dismissed them all as a group 'of visionary and impractical dreamers who conceived and acted a romantic drama, and applauded it, all by themselves'. As far as he was concerned, 'the Jews do not wish to and will not go back to Palestine'. When one compares the population of world Jewry in recent years with immigration rates to Israel since its establishment, it turns out that on this point Rabbi Wise was eminently correct.

There were, of course, American Jews in those years who embraced political Zionism with warmth and alacrity. Some of them even participated in the Basle Congress. But with only some 12,000 registered Zionists out of an American Jewish population of 3 million in 1914 they were obviously few in number, and they did not grow substantially in number until the terrible years of Adolf Hitler and the Nazi Holocaust of the 1940s.

One of their problems was handling the charge of dual loyalty – to America and to Zion. While it is difficult to find any evidence that Irish-Americans, Italian-Americans, or Lebanese-Americans (to name just three of the so-called hyphenated ethnic groups in the United States) have had their fellow ethnics impugn their loyalty to America for supporting the independence and territorial integrity of Ireland, Italy, and Lebanon, such is not the case with American Jewish supporters of Israel.

In 1899, during its annual convention, the New York Federation of Zionists felt compelled to adopt the following resolution : 'Resolved, that we declare our loyalty to the country in which we live, and that our aim in furthering Zionism is merely of a sympathetic nature . . .' [4] In 1907 Dr Harry Friedenwald, president of the American Federation of Zionists, also felt compelled to issue this statement : [5]

The opposition has reduced itself to a misstatement of our aims, to vituperation and defamation, to aspersions upon our fidelity to Judaism on the one hand and our loyalty to this country on the other . . . To be an American, we are told, requires that we must divest ourself of our Jewish all.

We answer that America requires nothing of the kind. There is a provision in our constitution that guarantees religious freedom, and no American [Christian] has for a moment questioned the right of the Jews to their hopes. *It has remained for the Jew to call his brother traitor* [Italics added]. Let them well weigh the words they have spoken. The argument followed to its logical conclusion brands with treachery every pious Jew who daily prays . . . for the return to Zion.

Let us put an end to this discussion concerning the patriotism of the Zionist. The most pious believers in the restoration, the most ardent workers for its consummation, have shown themselves in no way inferior to other Americans in devotion to this country.

But the non-Zionist Jews did not put an end to this discussion of the patriotism of Zionist Jews. On the contrary, they intensified it. Within weeks of Friedenwald's plea, the famous banker and philanthropist Jacob H. Schiff wrote a letter to Rabbi Solomon Schechter, founder of Conservative Judaism and president of its Jewish Theological Seminary, in which he said: 'Speaking as an American, I cannot for a moment concede that one can be at the same time a true American and an honest adherent of the Zionist movement.' Then he added that Zionists 'place a prior lien upon their citizenship, which, if there would be a possibility for their desire and plans to become effective, would prevent them from maintaining allegiance to the country of which they now claim to be good citizens'.[6] In another letter to Schechter five weeks later, Schiff wrote:[7]

When the Zionists, as they assumed to do at their recent meeting, speak for the Jewish race, they forget that a very large percentage of our co-religionists are not Zionists and that a considerable number even of orthodox Jews are thoroughly opposed to Zionism. The political doctrine brought forth and advocated by Zionism has nothing in common with the Jewish Messianic hope . . . Nowhere is there anything in Jewish Holy Scriptures which justifies agitation to re-establish a Jewish nation and State by human endeavor.

In the same letter Schiff also accused the Zionists of delaying the integration into American society of the newly arrived and arriving Jewish immigrants from Eastern Europe:

In our own country the agitation for a Jewish state is apt to retard the Americanization of thousands who, in recent years, have come among us, and whose success and happiness in this and coming generations, no less than the weal of the [American] State, must . . . depend upon the readiness with which the newcomers shall be able in their civic condition – as separate from their faith – to become absorbed into the American people.

Because of the very strong opposition of men like Jacob Schiff and Rabbi Isaac Mayer Wise, it is tempting to attribute American Zionism's weakness at the time to the power of the German-Jewish establishment. Tempting but not true. Zionism was weak. But this was because it had not yet won the allegiance of 'the other Jews' in America: the vastly larger, poorer group from Eastern Europe.

Most of them were recent immigrants or the children of recent immigrants. They were vaguely in favor of ending the homelessness of their erstwhile ghetto brethren who could not reach American shores. However, before they could feel concern about European Jews and the Zionist solution to their problems, the recent Jewish immigrants to America had to take care of some pressing personal needs on this side of the ocean. They had to get jobs. They had to find shelter for their families. They had to learn English. They had to put their children into the public schools. In short, they had to become Americanized – and they had to do it quickly without losing their Jewishness along the way.

All this was not easy. For these newer additions to the American melting pot (or pressure cooker) had a vexing concern. They had to get their non-Jewish neighbors to accept their definition of American freedom and American pluralism : the right to be just like everyone else in society, simultaneously with the right to be different from everyone else in society. Sometimes they had to fight for the right to be just like their non-Jewish neighbors (in, say, matters of economic and educational opportunity). At other times they had to fight for the right to be quite different from their non-Jewish neighbors (in, say, matters of religion and culture). When one is struggling so hard to have the majority accept one's right as a minority to be both different and the same, one does not always have the inclination and the energy to struggle for such lofty objectives as a separate sovereign state for Jews elsewhere.

This began to change with World War I. The convulsive revolution in Russia, the terrible casualties, the war's brutality and dislocation, and the promises of self-determination made by the British, the French, and the Americans – all combined to enable American Zionism to 'put Jewish aspirations abreast of the nationalist hopes of the Irish, the Czechs, the Poles, the Hindus, and many lesser groups'.[8] By 1915 we find an intercollegiate Zionist group being founded at Harvard University. In that same year we find Kentucky-born Louis D. Brandeis, the first Jew to serve on the Supreme Court, telling the Zionists in convention : 'Let us Americans . . . lead earnestly, courageously, and joyously in the struggle for the liberation of the Jewish People !' He added : 'American Jews have not only the right but the duty to act. We are free from political or civil disability, and are relatively prosperous . . . Whether the Jewish problem shall be solved depends primarily, not upon others, but upon us.'[9]

Unlike Jacob Schiff, who saw Zionism as an obstruction to Jewish assimilation into the American system, Brandeis viewed it positively. He once said :[10]

> My approach to Zionism was through Americanism. In time, practical experience and observation convinced me that Jews were by reason of their traditions and their character peculiarly fitted for the attainment of American ideals. Gradually it became clear to me that to be good Americans we must be better Jews, and to be better Jews we must become Zionists. Jewish life cannot be preserved and developed, assimilation cannot be averted, unless there be established in the fatherland a center from which the Jewish spirit may radiate and give to the Jews scattered throughout the world that inspiration which springs from the memories of a great past and the hope of a great future.

Whether Schiff was ever familiar with this passage by Brandeis is not clear. But in a speech in 1917, fearful that Jewish life would begin to diminish in both Western Europe and Bolshevik Russia, he did echo the Brandeis idea of a Jewish spiritual center in Palestine, though he chose a different word :[11]

> I am not a believer in a Jewish nation built on all kinds of isms, with egotism as the first, and agnosticism and aetheism as the others. But I am a believer in the Jewish people and in the mission of the Jew, and I believe that somewhere there should be a great reservoir of Jewish learning in which Jewish culture might be furthered and developed, unhampered by the materialism of the world, and might spread its beautiful ideals over the world.

Another famous and philanthropic anti-Zionist Jew whom World War I definitely transformed was Adolph Lewisohn, the donor of the City University's Lewisohn Stadium, where generations of New Yorkers were treated to free concerts of the highest calibre. His conversion to Zionism was complete. He said so and he said why, also in 1917 :[12]

> I think favorably of the establishment of a Jewish state in Palestine and hope that the League to Enforce Peace [which

became the League of Nations after the war] will include the Jewish nation among those small nationalities which ought to be liberated and protected. I was formerly not in sympathy with the Zionist movement, but since America has entered the world war for the express purpose, as President Wilson said, of protecting the rights of all nationalities, the Jews all over the world should, in my opinion, favor the establishment of the Jewish State in Palestine, which will be a center of Hebraic life and will have influence upon Judaism everywhere.

There were American Jews whose opposition to Zionism was not in the least softened by European Jewish suffering during and after World War I. On the contrary, they were frightened and bitter when Great Britain endorsed the concept of a Jewish homeland in Palestine in the midst of the war and when America and, later, the League of Nations endorsed the British endorsement.

At its 1918 convention the Central Conference of American Rabbis, the umbrella organization of the Reform rabbinate, welcomed the Balfour Declaration as an expression of gentile good will. But the reference to a Jewish homeland in the Holy Land was anathema to the rabbis. In that same year Dr David Phillipson, rabbi of the Rosedale Avenue Reform Temple in Cincinnati, answered still another letter from Jacob Schiff, who had by then become a Zionist in everything but name:[13]

We sympathize no less keenly with the [Jewish] sufferers [of World War I] than does this great-hearted co-religionist of ours, but we feel that the solution for this intolerable condition lies not in securing only one national home for Jews . . . but in having every land become a national home . . .

Our opposition to Zionism is due to our conviction that this movement in its political aspects is a distinct menace to the best interest of the Jews in this and other lands. Zionism sets Jews apart as a national group. We American Jews who . . . teach and believe that the Jews constitute a religious community and not a nation, are Americans in nationality and Jews in religion.

Rabbi Phillipson also disapproved of the solicitation by the Zionists of the views of American Congressmen. 'This injecting of a purely Jewish matter into American politics is proof positive of the danger of political Zionism', he said. Even accepting his own purely religious definition of Judaism, Phillipson was not being true to the realities of the American political process. For other religious groups in the United States – for example, Bible-Belt Protestants with regard to the theory of human evolution, Mormons with regard to polygamy, and Catholics with regard to abortion – have turned to the American political and legal system for support and remedies whenever they wished to.

The antagonism between 'old American' Jews from Central and Western Europe and 'newcomers' from elsewhere surfaced in a letter that Simon W. Rosedale, a former New York Attorney-General, wrote to Representative Rollin B. Sanford in December 1918. Rosedale told Sanford that Zionism 'does not have the general sympathy or approval of that large religious organization known as Reform Jews of America'. He contended that Reform Jews were the majority of the community before the influx from Eastern Europe of Zionist Jews who were introducing 'an undesirable hyphenism', which was 'inconsistent with untainted Americanism'.[14]

When President Wilson once made a statement supporting Zionist aims, he was presented with a petition signed by thirty prominent, mostly Jewish, citizens, including Henry Morgenthau, former American ambassador to Turkey, the already-mentioned Simon Rosedale, Max Senior, former president of the National Conference of Jewish Charities, Rabbi Henry Berkowitz, chairman of the Jewish Chataqua Society, and Adolph S. Ochs of the *New York Times*. Noting that in 1919 there were only 150,000 Zionists out of a Jewish population of $3\frac{1}{2}$ million, the signers made a number of anti-Zionist arguments, of which the following was the final one:[15]

Whether the Jews be regarded as a 'race' or as a 'religion' it is contrary to democratic principles for which the world war was waged to found a nation on either or both of these bases . . . A Jewish state involves fundamental limitations as to race and religion, else the term 'Jewish' means nothing. To unite Church and State, in any form, as under the old Jewish hierarchy, would be a leap backward of 2,000 years.

President Wilson was not impressed. But what impression did these and other anti-Zionists make upon other Christians, as they witnessed the verbal war over Zionism within the American Jewish community?

The American Federation of Labor passed a resolution favoring a Jewish Palestinian homeland, as it and other American unions have done regularly ever since. William Blackstone not only revived his 1891 petition to President Harrison for submission to President Wilson, but in 1916 he also got the Presbyterian General Assembly to come out in favor of a Jewish homeland in Palestine. In 1918 a Zionist congress in Philadelphia acclaimed Blackstone 'the Father of Zionism', and in that same year Blackstone told a Zionist mass meeting in Los Angeles : 'I am and for over thirty years have been an ardent advocate of Zionism.' [16]

In 1918 Dr Adolph Augustus Berle, a former professor of applied Christianity at Tufts College, near Boston, wrote a little book that ranks among the most pro-Zionist essays penned between the two World Wars. Published by Mitchell Kennerley of New York, it is called *The World Significance of a Jewish State* and dedicated to Justice Louis D. Brandeis, 'Exemplar and Leader of the Liberating Influence of the Jew in American Life, With Memories of Our Struggles in the Public Service'. The book begins :

> It is many years since the author of this little essay became interested in the subject . . . The Zionist movement, as such, has interest chiefly for Jews. But the history of the Jews is a human possession, priceless because of its influence upon the moral and religious conceptions of men. This essay . . . [therefore] considers the proposed Jewish state for its significance to the Christian world.

Berle not only discussed and argued the Christian significance of a Jewish state. He actively pleaded for Christian support in making that state a practical reality. He could 'think of no greater contribution to the world's life than the religious rehabilitation and unification of the Jews'. And because a Jewish state looked to him like the best means of achieving this rehabilitation and unification, Berle asked 'the Christian world to supplement, with generous enthusiasm, this national aspiration of devoted Jews, that Americans may join . . . in bringing their influence to bear upon our own government, toward the fulfillment of so worthy an international end'.

On the other side of the gentile ledger, there was the steady anti-Zionism of *The Christian Century*, perhaps the most prestigious journal of American high church Protestantism. It warned against the 'Second Coming propaganda' of the premillennial and more fundamentalist groups who connected Christ's return with Israel's restoration in Palestine. It spoke out against encouraging 'aggressive Jews to claim the country as a "homeland" for their people'. It said that 'historically the Jew has never been in possession of Palestine'. And, for good measure, it relied on 'most modern Biblical scholars' for its contention that the Jewish Bible 'contains no anticipation of the restoration of Israel to its ancient homeland which can apply to the Jewish people and the present age.' [17]

As far as political figures were concerned, former President William Howard Taft made a speech during World War I in which he stated that some definitive solution to the Jewish problem had to be placed on the agenda of the postwar peace conference. Taft's successor, Woodrow Wilson, under whom America entered the war, considered himself a Zionist. But for a while he was constrained from saying so too publicly. This was because while the United States had declared war on Germany in 1917 it had not done so against Turkey, Germany's ally and Palestine's ruler. To have commented too often and publicly on the postwar disposition of territory belonging to a nation with which America was at peace, was something Wilson could not do – at least not until the issuance of the Balfour Declaration, on 2 November 1917.

This Middle Eastern milestone, which Israelis celebrate and Arabs curse, came in the form of a letter from Arthur James Balfour, the British Foreign Secretary, to Lord Rothschild, the president of the British Zionist Federation : [18]

> I have much pleasure in conveying to you, on behalf of His Majesty's Government, the following declaration of sympathy with Jewish Zionist aspirations which has been submitted to, and approved by, the Cabinet.
>
> 'His Majesty's Government view with favour the establishment in Palestine of a national home for the Jewish people, and will use their best endeavours to facilitate the achievement of this object, it being clearly understood that nothing shall be done which may prejudice the civil and religious rights of existing non-Jewish communities in Palestine, or the rights and political status enjoyed by Jews in any other country.'
>
> I should be grateful if you would bring this declaration to the knowledge of the Zionist Federation.

We know that Britain was in touch with Wilson about the issuance of the Declaration and that various drafts were shown to him in order to get his prior approval. Additionally, according to Richard H. S. Crossman, a former Labour Member of Parliament, a member of the 1946 Anglo-American committee of inquiry on Palestine, and a gentile Zionist, Balfour, in his discussions in the Cabinet about Britain's association with a Jewish national home, 'concentrated entirely on the propaganda advantages of issuing the Declaration at once, arguing that it would win support among the Jews in America, as well as rallying the Jews in Russia against the Bolsheviks'.[19]

Whether or not that was actually the case, the State Department was adamantly opposed to American approval and probably would have opposed any draft of any official policy statement favoring Zionist aims. We know, too, that Colonel Edward House, Wilson's adviser in the White House, informed London on 11 September 1917 that the President felt that the issuance of a declaration was inopportune. If Britain felt it had to issue one anyway it should, said House, go no 'further perhaps than one of sympathy, provided it could be made without conveying any real commitment'.[20]

We also know that on 23 September 1917 Louis Brandeis, the American Zionist leader, cabled Chaim Weizmann, the British and world Zionist leader: 'From talks I have had with the President and from expressions of opinion given to closest advisors I feel that I can answer that he is in entire sympathy with the [proposed British] declaration quoted in yours of the 19th'.[21]

Wilson was. And he finally said so publicly in a letter to Rabbi Stephen S. Wise, vice-president of the Zionist Organization of America, in August 1918 : 'I welcome an opportunity to express the satisfaction I have felt in the progress of the Zionist movement in the United States and in the allied countries since the declaration by Mr Balfour on behalf of the British Government.'[22]

President Wilson was not the only American politician who endorsed the Balfour Declaration. Many members of Congress did. Among the more powerful were Champ Clark, Speaker of the House of Representatives, and Henry Cabot Lodge, chairman of the Senate Foreign Relations Committee. While Lodge torpedoed Wilson's work by successfully opposing America's signing of the Versailles Peace Treaty and its joining the League of Nations, he marched along with Wilson on the question of a Jewish political presence in Palestine. In response to a set of questions which the

Zionist Organization of America sent to him, as well as to all other members of Congress, Lodge wrote :[23]

> I should be glad to see action by the United States Government in line with the British Declaration . . . I should favor the adoption of an appropriate resolution by Congress in favor of the establishment in Palestine of a Jewish National Centre.
>
> I feel that the effort of the Jewish people to establish a National Home in Palestine is not only natural but in all ways to be desired.

Senator Lodge represented the state of Massachusetts, which in 1918, according to the *American Jewish Year Book* for that year, contained 189,671 Jews out of a total population of 3,832,790. This was a relatively large percentage (nearly 5 percent), although it is doubtful that this weighed heavily in Senator Lodge's decision to write what he wrote. But in Colorado, Maine, and Iowa there were tiny number of Jews in 1918, respectively 14,565 out of 1,014,581; 7,387 out of 782,191; and 15,555 out of 2,224,771. So that neither the friends nor the foes of Zionism can really explain the extremely pro-Zionist responses of Senators from those states on the basis of electoral considerations. There just were not enough Jews living in them to make a difference, even if every Jew voted and even if every Jew voted for the men who made the responses.

Senator Charles S. Thomas of Colorado believed that returning Palestine to the Jews would not only be just but would also be politically beneficial to the United States. And he thought that 'the effort of the Jewish people to establish a national home in Palestine should be encouraged at all times'. Senator Frederick Hale of Maine, in his reply to the Zionist Organization of America, said: 'I thoroughly approve of the actions of our allies on the Zionist question. The restoration to the Jews of their old homeland is an act of justice that the world owes them . . . By returning Palestine to the Jews, the allied powers are carrying out a sacred duty.'

Notice something very significant here. In the Balfour Declaration the British very deliberately declared their intention to support the establishment only of a Jewish *home in* Palestine. From the Declaration itself one cannot tell whether they meant a home in a tiny portion of Palestine, in a very large part of it, or in all of it. By using the phrases 'the restoration to the Jews of their old homeland' and 'returning Palestine to the Jews', Senator Hale went much farther than the British and even most Zionists of the time. Indeed, his colleague from Iowa, Albert B. Cummins, went the farthest of all: 'If it be the desire of the Jewish people themselves, I am in favor of lending our national influence toward the establishment in Palestine of a government; that is to say, an independent state.'

In order to help him make up his mind about the final American position with regard to Palestine at the peace conference in Versailles, Woodrow Wilson commissioned two studies. One was by the intelligence section of the American negotiating team at Versailles. The other was by Henry C. King, president of Oberlin College, and Charles R. Crane, a Chicagoan with many business connections in the Middle East, especially with Turkey, from which Britain had conquered Palestine in 1917.

King and Crane, together with a few technical advisers, were asked to visit parts of the former Ottoman Empire and:

> to acquaint themselves . . . with the shade of opinion there . . . with the social, racial, and economic conditions . . . and to form as definite an opinion as the circumstances and the time at your disposal will permit, as to the division of territory and assignment of mandates.

Regarding territorial disposition, they recommended that Palestine and Lebanon be treated as part of Syria and that the mandate (or non-self-governing trusteeship) over this Greater Syria be given to the British only if the Americans could not secure it for themselves. As for the Jewish connection to the area, the King–Crane Commission declared that the Zionist claim 'that they have a "right" to Palestine, based on an occupation of two thousand years ago, can hardly be seriously considered'. For this and other reasons, including the opposition of most Christians and Muslims in and around Palestine, the commission recommended 'that Jewish immigration to Palestine should definitely be limited and that the project for making Palestine distinctly a Jewish commonwealth should be given up'.[24]

The report of the intelligence section of the American Commission to Negotiate Peace at Versailles took a different tack altogether. Its recommendations were:[25]

(1) That there be established a separate state of Palestine.

(2)   That this state be placed under Great Britain as a mandatory of the League of Nations.

(3)   That the Jews be invited to return to Palestine and settle there, being assured by the [Peace] Conference of all proper assistance in so doing that may be consistent with the protection of the personal (especially the religious) and the property rights of the non-Jewish population, and being further assured that it will be the policy of the League of Nations to recognize Palestine as a Jewish state as soon as it is a Jewish state in fact.

(4)   That the holy places and religious rights of all creeds in Palestine be placed under the protection of the League of Nations and its mandatory.

The intelligence section's sympathy for Zionist aspirations is especially marked in one paragraph of the 'Discussion' portion of its report, which reads :

> It is right that Palestine should become a Jewish state, if the Jews, being given the full opportunity, make it such. It was the cradle and home of their vital race, which has made large spiritual contributions to mankind, and is the only land in which they can hope to find a home of their own; they being in this last respect unique among significant peoples.

For reasons unknown, the King–Crane Report was never submitted to the Paris peace conference; it was not even published until some years after it. But while Wilson did not come out for Jewish statehood he did, in a visit back to America during the conference, tell a Jewish group, for publication, that he 'was persuaded that the Allied nations, with the fullest concurrence of our own Government and people, are agreed that in Palestine there shall be laid the foundation of a Jewish commonwealth'.[26]

Words have meanings and connotations, and speakers of the same language may differ over them. But it seems that if commonwealth means less than state, it also means more than homeland. In any event, American Zionists were quite pleased with Wilson's role, which Professor Selig Adler, a leading specialist in the subject, sums up this way :[27]

There can be no doubt that Wilson's approval of the Balfour

Declaration and his subsequent stand on the promise greatly strengthened the hands of the Zionists and were influential in securing the final settlement. Without the American President's intervention, the Zionists might have received much less than they did. Wilson's stand is remarkable, because it was opposed by almost all who surrounded him – Colonel House, [Secretary of State] Robert Lansing, the balance of his American colleagues in Paris, the King–Crane Commission, the Near Eastern Division of the State Department, and our consular representatives in Palestine and the vicinity. The name of Woodrow Wilson belongs among the 'fathers' of the new commonwealth of Israel.

6

Twentieth-Century Zionism: from Jewish Home to Jewish Commonwealth

The British ruled Palestine for thirty years, from 1918 to 1948. During the first five years they ruled it *de facto* as a result of General Sir Edmund Allenby's rout of Turkish forces in the area toward the end of World War I. Their *de jure* rule began in 1922, when the newly formed League of Nations, recognizing 'the historical connection of the Jewish people with Palestine', awarded it to Great Britain with the understanding that the 'Mandatory shall be responsible for placing the country under such political, administrative and economic conditions as will secure the establishment of the Jewish national home'.[1] The British ended their stay in 1948, some six months after the United Nations (which had succeeded the League as world security organization) recommended an internationalized Jerusalem and the partition of what was left of the original Palestine of 1922 into two separate and independent states – one Arab, the other Jewish.

In the interim there were struggles among the British, the Arabs, and the Jews, the consequences of which often spilled over into the American political and diplomatic arena. In fact, during the entire generation of British rule in Palestine Americans maintained a lively interest in what took place there. In this they were pushed along by the deteriorating 'twenty-year truce' between the end of World War I and the beginning of World War II, and by the terrible events of World War II itself.

American interest in Palestine was maintained by several overlapping and interacting groups. One was the private citizens and bodies, both Jewish and non-Jewish, who fought the public opinion battle on the side of the Zionists. Another was those citizens and organizations, including the anti-Zionist American Council for Judaism, who fought it on the other side. A third group was the politicians. From Presidents to Congressmen and from governors to mayors, they constantly tested the political winds to see which way they were blowing with reference to Jews and to Zionism. The State Department did the same with the winds of foreign policy. And whenever America's diplomats could safely ignore or bend the wishes of the President and the Congress, they usually came down on the side of the Arabs. All this was taking place during the rise of fascism and Nazism in the 1920s, the persecution of the Jews of Germany and Austria in the 1930s, the murder of 6 million Jews by the Germans and their non-Aryan helpers in occupied Europe in the 1940s, and the pressure to 'do something' for the emaciated survivors – euphemistically called displaced persons or DPs – when World War II finally ended in an allied victory over the Axis powers in 1945.

The reemergence of traditional American isolationism and the fear that League membership would automatically involve it in all sorts of foreign entanglements prevented the United States from ever joining the League of Nations. But because it had fought on the victorious side in the war that gave birth to the organization, it claimed the right to approve all mandates, including the one for Palestine. Great Britain accepted America's assertion of that right in a 1924 treaty which promised protection of American interests in Palestine. It also promised that no modification in the original terms of the mandate would be made without prior American consent. That last promise became a bone of contention later, when the British, trying to meet what they considered their responsibility toward the Palestinian Arabs, placed heavy immigration and other restrictions upon Jews wishing to enter Palestine.

But that was in 1939. In the more hope-filled days of 1922 the House of Representatives and the Senate unanimously passed, and President Warren G. Harding signed, a Joint Resolution that resolved that 'the United States of America favors the establishment in Palestine of a national home for the Jewish people'.[2] Earlier, when the chairman of the World Zionist Executive met with Harding on a trip to America, he announced, as reported in the *New York Times* of 25 November 1921 : 'I am happy to state that there has been no change of policy of the United States Government toward Zionism. The present President, Mr Harding, sympathizes with us.' Harding used his own words to voice his public support in May 1922, when he stated : 'I am very glad to express my approval and hearty sympathy for the effort . . . in behalf of the restoration of Palestine as a homeland for the Jewish people'.[3] In June 1924 Harding's successor, Calvin Coolidge, added his name to the list of American chief executives in favor of Zionist aspirations.

The President between Coolidge and Franklin Delano Roosevelt was Herbert Hoover, who served from 1929 to 1933. In the library that houses his presidential papers at West Branch, Iowa, there is a copy of a letter he wrote on 29 August 1929 to the Zionist Organization of America. The ZOA had asked him for a statement on the Arab massacre of the Jews of Hebron, which had occurred earlier that year. Hoover said he was sure that the British would restore order. But in an attached memorandum he also made his first public statement about what the Jews were doing in the Holy Land:

> I have watched with keen interest and sympathy the splendid work for the upbuilding of Palestine, in which so many American Jews take an important part, in behalf of their less fortunate brethren abroad. It is a historic task . . . The Holy Land, desolate and neglected for centuries, is being rebuilt not only as an inspiring spiritual center, but also as a habitable and peaceful land that will in the near future harbor a large population with increased opportunities for prosperity among the farmers, the industrialists, the laborers and the scholars.

Just before leaving the presidency, Hoover wrote to the chairman of the American Palestine Campaign, again commending the work being done to build the Jewish homeland. 'Your efforts', he added, 'hold universal significance to Jewry, even as the Jewish people have made a world contribution to spiritual advancement.'[4]

From these two documents it is clear that Hoover was a friend of Zionism before and after Hitler's rise. But no mention of him in connection with the Jews and Arabs of Palestine can be made without also mentioning his unique scheme, first published on 19 November 1945 by the *New York World-Telegram,* for resettling Palestine's Arabs in Iraq.[5] The plan can be judged objectively, on its merits and demerits, or subjectively, in accordance with one's biases and perceptions. But it cannot be ignored. It cannot be ignored because it was conceived and promoted by an American President who was no longer in office, who was not Jewish, who was never personally involved in the Zionist movement, and who was no longer active in politics when he proposed his plan. While the Hoover Presidential Papers contain a letter showing that Eleanor Roosevelt thought well of the plan, there are no indications that any other American President, including her husband, who succeeded Herbert Hoover, ever endorsed so radical and unjust a solution to the Palestine problem.

As for Franklin Delano Roosevelt (popularly known as FDR), no other Chief Executive was so trustingly beloved by American Jews; no other Chief Executive disappointed them so. FDR's term in office (1933–45) coincided with Adolf Hitler's term in office. In other words, Roosevelt was President during Hitler's rising tyranny; during World War II, when there was a desperate need for the Jews of Germany and occupied Europe to find life-saving places of refuge in America, Palestine, and elsewhere; and at the time of the physical destruction of European Jewry – one-third of the entire Jewish population of the world. Yet the response of the Roosevelt administration to those twelve years of unspeakable horror was easy talk surrounded by total inaction.

For all his supposedly close friendship with the great American Zionist leader, Rabbi Stephen S. Wise, and despite the many pro-Zionist statements he made to Wise and to others, Roosevelt's record on Zionism and the plight of the doomed Jews of Europe is full of duplicity and deceit. He matched almost every encouraging public pronouncement to the Jews with an equally encouraging secret message to the Arabs, in effect promising them a veto over any final disposition of the Palestine problem that was not to their liking.

In the face of all the horrible things he knew were happening and were likely to happen, Roosevelt did nothing to get persecuted Jews into America or to pressure Britain into letting more of them into Palestine. He did not push Congress to liberalize, if only temporarily, America's then racist and anti-Semitic immigration laws. He did not even suggest that the unused immigration quotas assigned to the United Kingdom, Germany, Scandinavia, and so on, be redistributed so that Jews might enter America without raising the total legal limit for foreign immigrants for any one year. He did not instruct American consuls in Europe (as Hitler's semi-ally, fascist General Francisco Franco, instructed Spanish consuls) to make the most lenient administrative interpretations possible of America's visa-granting procedures and immigration laws. He did not give strong, early, and believable warnings to the leaders of Germany that they would be held accountable for the genocide being committed daily in their names and under their orders. He did not do everything he could have (before 1944 at least) to release funds and transport to save those Jews that could still be saved. He never ordered the pinpoint bombing of the Nazi death and concentration camps and roads and rail lines leading to and from them. And he most certainly did not push the British to rescind the 1939 White Paper – about which more later – and let Jews who could reach Palestine enter a country entrusted to the British for the supposed purpose of establishing and securing a Jewish national home. (From the Zionist viewpoint, what good is a national home if you cannot get into it when you need it most?)

When his own wife protested to him about his penchant for letting his pragmatism overwhelm his principles, he would tell her : 'First things come first, and I can't alienate votes I need for measures that are more important at the moment by pushing any measure that would entail a fight.' In her book *This I Remember* Mrs Roosevelt also wrote : 'While I often felt strongly on various subjects, Franklin frequently refrained from supporting causes in which he believed, because of political realities.' [6] One of those realities was America's fear of more Jewish immigrants – based in no small measure on outright anti-Semitism – and poll after poll taken during the period prove that Roosevelt was measuring public opinion on this issue quite correctly.

Some specific examples and consequences of the Roosevelt style regarding Jews, Zionism, and Palestine stand out in particular. The first example occurred in 1938, when Roosevelt encouraged the calling of a conference to deal with the ever more persecuted Jews of Nazi Germany. It took place at Evian-les-Bains on the French side of Lake Geneva. Not only did the Americans at Evian fail to persuade practically anyone else to do anything about the victims of Nazi persecution but all they themselves did was announce that America was going to accept into its midst the full combined annual quota of German and Austrian Jewish refugees. Assuming that the refugees managed to reach America before the Gestapo got them, this would amount to a total of 27,370 people.

Obviously, neither Roosevelt nor his surrogates – and one must remember that, more than most American Presidents, FDR was his own *de facto* Secretary of State – were very moved by what the conservative *New York Times* columnist Anne O'Hare McCormick wrote on the eve of the conference : [7]

It is heartbreaking to think of the queues of desperate human beings around our consulates in Vienna and other cities waiting in suspense for what happens at Evian. But the question they underline is not simply humanitarian. It is not a question of how many unemployed this country can safely add to its own unemployed millions. It is a test of civilization . . . Can America live with itself if it lets Germany get away with this policy of extermination, allows the fanaticism of one man to triumph over reason, refuses even to take up this gage of battle against barbarism?

Roosevelt did not take up the gage of battle even when it was thrown at him by the barbarian himself. For on the eve of the Evian Conference Hitler said at Konigsberg :[8]

I can only hope and expect that the other world, which has such deep sympathy of these [Jewish] criminals, will at least be generous enough to convert this sympathy into practical aid. We, on our part, are ready to put all these criminals at the disposal of those countries, for all I care, even on luxury ships.

Indeed the second Roosevelt-related event concerned a ship, the Hamburg-America Line's *St Louis*. On 13 May 1939 it left Germany for Havana with 936 passengers. All but six of them had proper American immigration visas. The only technicality – and it turned out to be a deadly one for the passengers – was that the visas were validated for dates ranging from three days to three months after their arrival and temporary stay in Cuba. But when the ship arrived in Havana, despite the belief of the passengers that they had valid Cuban transit visas in their possession, the Cubans allowed only twenty-eight of them to disembark. One attempted suicide, leaping over the side. The Cubans let him stay, but not the members of his family, who were left on board. Aside from him, no one was allowed to leave the vessel, and no amount of urging from anybody anywhere could budge the Cubans from their stance.

Finally, the sympathetic shipmaster, Captain Gustav Schroeder, headed the *St Louis* to America, where it sailed along the East Coast for days. The passengers saw Miami from the railing. But if nothing and no one could budge the Cuban authorities in Havana, nothing and no one could budge the American authorities in Washington either. Not even a personal message to FDR from the passengers themselves helped. Although their cable to the President poignantly noted that more than 400 of the remaining 907 passengers were women and children, neither FDR nor any government official acting on his behalf cabled back a single word of reply. (How different was the response of President Carter in 1980, when thousands upon thousands of refugees from Castro's Cuba were allowed into the United States.)

No longer able to delay returning to Europe, Captain Schroeder headed homeward on 6 June 1939, barely three months before the outbreak of World War II. Some 280 passengers ultimately got to Britain, the rest to Belgium, Holland, and France. But with Hitler's invasions of the latter countries, no one knows how many of the others perished and how many survived. When the Nazis heard of the saga of the *St Louis*, they gloated with unabashed glee. The August 1939 issue of *Der Weltkampf* (The World Struggle) wrote: 'We are saying openly that we do not want the Jews while the democracies keep on claiming that they are willing to receive them – and then leave the guests out in the cold! Aren't we savages better men after all?' [9]

On 16 December 1941 – nine days after the Japanese attack on Pearl Harbor and America's entry into the war – another ship, a small, 180-ton vessel, the *Struma*, set sail from the Romanian Black Sea port of Constanta with a human cargo of 769 Jewish refugees. It was bound for Haifa. But because the *Struma* was overloaded and defective to begin with it broke down off Istanbul. Without immigration certificates for Palestine, which the passengers did not have and which the mandatory officials refused to send them, the Turks refused to let the passengers land. Instead, they towed the leaky little boat out to sea. Six miles off the Turkish coast it sank. Some say it hit a mine. Some say it was torpedoed by a German submarine. Some say it capsized. Some say it simply fell apart. No matter. Only two people managed to begin the swim back to shore and only one of them actually made it. All the rest of the *Struma*'s passengers, including 70 children and 269 women, drowned.

As a result of violent Arab–Jewish disturbances in 1936 between the two groups in Palestine, and because the British were still trying to build some workable bridge between them, London sent out a Royal Commission, usually known as the Peel Commission, after its chairman, Earl Peel. Noting that neither 'Arab nor Jew has any sense of service to a single state', the Peel Commission concluded that 'the disease [from which Palestine is suffering] is so deep rooted that ... the only hope of a cure lies in a surgical operation'.

Specifically, the Commission recommended a three-way partition of the country into a Jewish state, an Arab one, and an area that would continue to remain under British control. Nothing came of the scheme because the principle of partition received only limited support from the League of Nations, the British Parliament, and the Jews – and none from the Arabs.

In retrospect it is obvious that the British had allowed the exigencies and expediencies of World War I to place them in an impossible and contradictory position. They made conflicting promises to two groups of people over the same piece of territory. Even the carefully worded Balfour Declaration is a contradiction because it called for a Jewish home in Palestine that would not prejudice the civil and religious rights of the Arabs already living there. Besides, at no time did the bulk of Palestine's Arabs or their leaders ever agree to their eventual transformation from a majority to a minority of the country's population as a result of Jewish immigration. So as the clouds of World War II began to gather over Nazi Germany and over Europe generally, Britain announced a radical shift in its Palestine policy with the issuance of the White Paper of May 1939.

In it a new objective was declared : not a Jewish national home in Palestine but the establishment within a decade of an independent binational Palestinian state. To accomplish this objective the following steps were to be taken. First, constitutional reforms would be instituted to give both the Jewish and Arab Palestinians – in those days all legal residents of Palestine were known as Palestinians – 'an increasing part in the government of their own country'. Secondly, between 1939 and 1944 (regardless of what was happening or might happen to the Jews of Europe during those years) Jewish immigration would be limited to 75,000 persons, after which time 'no further Jewish immigration will be permitted unless the Arabs of Palestine [who were still the vast majority of the population] are prepared to acquiesce in it'. Thirdly, the Palestine government would be granted powers to prohibit and regulate further land transfers from Arab to Jewish ownership. The war forced Britain to postpone the program of constitutional reform. However, restrictions on Jewish immigration and Jewish land purchase were strictly enforced.[10]

Two months before the White Paper came out, when reports reached Washington that London was contemplating its change in the mandate, twenty-eight American Senators inserted into the

Congressional Record a statement expressing the 'hope that the spirit and the letter of the Balfour declaration [as it applied to the building of a Jewish national home in Palestine] be preserved in all its integrity'. On 25 May – eight days after the White Paper's issuance – fifteen members of the Foreign Affairs Committee of the House of Representatives did the same thing, making the additional point that Britain's new policy was a violation of the 1924 Convention between Great Britain and the United States, especially article 7 which provided for no changes in the terms of the original Palestine mandate without American assent. According to the members of the House of Representatives, such assent was neither asked for nor given.

What was the reaction of the State Department to all of this? In a very long statement published in the 13 October 1938 issue of the *New York Times* the Department noted that (1) it had received a large number of letters and telegrams from American individuals and organizations concerning the proposed changes in the mandate; (2) every American President since Wilson had expressed interest in and pleasure at the progress of the Jewish national home in Palestine; (3) a September 1922 Joint Resolution of Congress had indeed endorsed the idea of such a homeland; and (4) article 7 of the 1924 Convention did give the United States some rights with respect to changes in the terms of the Palestine mandate, as did corresponding articles in other treaties signed by the United States with respect to mandated territories elsewhere. It was, however, the Department's legal opinion that 'None of these articles empower the Government of the United States to prevent the modification of the terms of any of the mandates'.

Zionists and Israelis have never considered the Department of State to be a bastion of support for either Jewish Palestine or the Israeli state. On the contrary, its pro-Arabism has been commented upon *ad nauseam*, especially by Zionists. It is thus fashionable, particularly in certain Diaspora Zionist and Israeli circles, to blame the professionals in the Department for *every* downturn in American–Israeli relations. But, as already pointed out, Franklin D. Roosevelt was his own chief diplomat. If anyone wishes to blame the Department alone for the official American response to the 1939 White Paper and to British policy in Palestine during World War II, he is free to do so. But that would take President Roosevelt off the hook and would be unfair to the State Department, especially to those who were more kindly disposed to Jewish self-determination in the Holy Land. In any case, if Roosevelt and his State Department could not see the link between Zionist ideology, the persecuted Jews of Europe and the fate of the Jewish national home, others could – not only with regard to the White Paper but to other Palestine-related issues before and after the war.

In 1927, for example, Dr Harry Emerson Fosdick, pastor of New York's Riverside Church and a professor at Union Theological Seminary, published a book about Palestine. In it he was of two minds on Zionism. On the one hand, he worried about Jewish 'chauvinistic nationalism' in a country which was then three-quarters Arab. On the other, he wrote that 'while tragedy is obviously possible, I personally hope that Zionism may succeed'. For Fosdick Zionism's driving force was

> not difficult even for a non-Jew to understand. The patriotism of the Jews for Palestine has a long tradition. This long cherished dream of restoration . . . has become the more alluring to Jewish people as the hardships of their life elsewhere . . . have shut against them other doors of hope. The treatment of the Jews in Christendom makes one of the most appalling stories of truculence and bigotry that history knows.[11]

Two years later, Fosdick's fellow Christian churchman, John Haynes Holmes, the minister of New York's Community Church for forty-two years, published an extremely pro-Zionist book in which he wrote: 'What the Jew is seeking in Zion is not only his country but his soul', and Holmes was certain that in Palestine he would find both. But Holmes was very wary of Britain's true intentions in the Holy Land – much more so and much sooner, it seems, than Jewish Zionists like Dr Chaim Weizmann, for instance. Only seven years after Britain's acquisition of the Palestine mandate from the League, ten years before the 1939 White Paper, and twenty years before Israel's establishment as a state Holmes wrote in his book:

> At bottom these two groups, the Mandatory and Zion, are not interested at all in the same things. Whatever may be the words of the Balfour Declaration, or the Jewish interpretation of these words, it remains a fact that the English did not go to Palestine, and are not now remaining there, for the purpose . . . of establishing a 'national home for the Jewish people'.

On the contrary, the English went to Palestine, as they have gone to many other remote places . . . simply and solely to safeguard the interests of British power throughout the world . . . [Their] concern is not with Zion but with Empire.' [12]

One of Jewish Palestine's most staunch supporters was Dr Walter Clay Lowdermilk, assistant chief of the soil conservation service of the United States Department of Agriculture. In the 1930s he traveled to about twenty countries all over the world in order to study how each generation used its land and in what condition it passed it on to the next generation. When Lowdermilk reached Palestine he was completely enchanted by what he saw the Jews doing with their land. So impressed was he that he wrote an article in the January 1940 issue of *American Forests*, the professional journal of the American Forestry Association. In September 1942 the article was revised and reprinted in *The Christian Rural Fellowship Bulletin*. It contains Lowdermilk's Eleventh Commandment.

If Moses had foreseen what was to become of the [Promised Land] and vast areas of wasted lands, such as we have seen in China, Korea, North Africa, Asia Minor, Mesopotamia and our own United States; namely, the wastage of land due to suicidal agriculture and the resulting man-made deserts and ruined civilizations, if he had foreseen the impoverishment, revolutions, wars, migrations, and social decadence of billions of people through thousands of years and the oncoming desolation of their lands, he doubtless would have been inspired to deliver an 'Eleventh' Commandment to complete the trinity of man's responsibilities – to his Creator, to his fellow men, and to Mother Earth. Such a commandment should read somewhat as follows :

XI Thou shalt inherit the holy earth as a faithful steward, conserving its resources and productivity from generation to generation. Thou shalt safeguard thy fields from soil erosion, thy living waters from drying up, thy forests from desolation, and protect the hills from overgrazing by thy herds, that thy descendents may have abundance forever. If any shall fail in this stewardship of the land thy fruitful fields shall become sterile stony ground and wasting gullies, and thy descendents shall decrease and live in poverty or perish from off the face of the earth.

This ecological-environmentalist view transformed Lowdermilk into an ardent Zionist. (His 1944 book, *Palestine: Land of Promise*, was a bestseller, which may reveal something more about the predilection of the American public for the achievement of Zionist aims in the Holy Land.) But the Eleventh Commandment also has a potentially dangerous cast to it – even for Zionism and for Israel. It posits a people's right to sovereignty not on their historical, cultural, religious, and political claims to a piece of land, but on what they do with it. This 'making-the-deserts-bloom' argument sounds good and the Jews have often used it. But it really weakens their more valid claims to renewed sovereignty because it may be used against them if they should ever fall below some arbitrary norm of what is and what is not proper agricultural and technological use of the land and its resources. Moreover, the Lowdermilk concept, though well intentioned, is a potential danger to *any* country in the world which happens to be, at least in Western eyes, agriculturally and technologically backward. It is simply an unacceptable standard for the achievement or continuation of state sovereignty. Nevertheless, there was at least one other American Christian of the period, the writer Dorothy Thompson, who accepted it. In a March 1944 address she said : [13]

The Jews of Zion have kept His Commandments . . . And as long as they keep on building, as long as the creative spirit moves them in their great trek toward Palestine, he who stands in the way is halting the whole progress of man into the only true liberation.

Several pro-Zionist Christian groups emerged in the 1930s and 1940s, often with Jewish organizational and financial support. One was the American Palestine Committee, whose announced objective was 'to organize more effectively our endeavors as non-Jews to cooperate with this great idealistic cause' and 'to foster the development of an informed public opinion in the United States among non-Jews concerning Zionist activities, purposes, and achievements in Palestine'.[14] After being fairly inactive for a decade, the committee was reconstituted and revitalized in March 1941 under the chairmanship of Democratic Senator Robert F. Wagner of New York, and Republican Senator Charles F. McNary of Oregon, a state with relatively few Jews. One of its vice-chairmen was William Green, president of the American Federation of Labor. Altogether,

the initial membership of the American Palestine Committee totaled
over 700 people, including scores of Christian clergymen, twenty-
two state governors, 200 Congressmen (or about half of the House
of Representatives), sixty-eight Senators (or about two-thirds of the
Senate), and three Cabinet members. The Congressional contingent
comprised the Senate Majority Leader, the Speaker of the House
of Representatives, the chairman of the Senate Foreign Relations
Committee, the House Majority Leader, and the House Minority
Leader.

Another non-Jewish Zionist group was the Christian Council on
Palestine, formed in December 1942. Among its founders were the
famous Protestant theologian Reinhold Niebuhr, his equally famous
colleague, Paul Tillich, Henry A. Atkinson, general secretary of the
Church Peace Union, the already-mentioned John Haynes Holmes,
Daniel A. Poling, editor of the *Christian Herald,* and the renowned
Biblical archeologist Professor William F. Albright. After the war the
two groups – the American Palestine Committee and the Christian
Council on Palestine – merged into a larger, more effective organi-
zation known as the American Christian Palestine Committee
(ACPC).

In 1944 Senator Wagner and his Republican colleague and
fellow ACPC member, Robert A. Taft, introduced a Congressional
resolution resolving that:[15]

the United States shall use its good offices and take appropriate
measures to the end that the doors of Palestine shall be opened
for free entry of Jews into that country, and that there shall
be a full opportunity for colonization, so that the Jewish people
may ultimately reconstitute Palestine as a free and democratic
Jewish commonwealth.

By the end of 1944 the overwhelming majority of the members
of both Houses had expressed themselves in favor of the bipartisan
Wagner–Taft Resolution. Yet it was not acted upon because the
War Department insisted that its passage would hinder the winning
of the war.

To counter the arguments of Christian anti-Zionists, especially
the editors of *The Christian Century,* as well as the successful efforts
of the military people to squelch not only the Wagner–Taft Resolution but all pro-Zionist resolutions before Congress, Reinhold
Niebuhr argued in the 3 April issue of *Christianity and Crisis,* that

Christians who do not believe that the White Paper restriction on immigration to Palestine should be abrogated, as advocated by a pending senatorial resolution, ought to feel obligated to state a workable alternative. The homeless Jews must find a home, and Christians owe their Jewish brethren something more than verbal sympathy . . . The fact that General [George C.] Marshall [the Army Chief of Staff and closest military advisor to President Roosevelt] has intervened in the debate about immigration to Palestine, because in his belief, senatorial action might interfere with the strategy of oil pipelines to Arabia, raises an issue . . . To what degree shall problems of political justice be subordinated to necessities of military strategy?

Because Zionist leaders in Nazi-occupied Europe were being slaughtered and those in Palestine were both cooperating with the British because of Hitler and in conflict with them because of the White Paper, the locus of Zionist public relations and diplomatic activity shifted to the United States. The shift was symbolized by an Extraordinary Zionist Conference at New York's Biltmore Hotel in May 1942, convened by the four largest American Zionist groups – the Zionist Organization of America, Hadassah (the Women's Zionist Organization of America), the Mizrachi (the religious Zionists), and the Labor Zionists, who were closely tied to the socialist and kibbutz-oriented party that dominated the Jewish community of Palestine.

The significance of the Biltmore Conference was that (1) the world Zionist movement finally declared that Jewish aspirations in Palestine had no hope of achievement under the British mandatory regime; (2) the official aim of the movement was no longer a Jewish home but a Jewish commonwealth; (3) at least until the end of the war, the leadership of the movement would be in the hands of North American Jews, especially the anti-British Rabbi Abba Hillel Silver of Cleveland; and (4) what might be called the Zionization of the American Jewish community had begun to enter its final phase. True, there were anti-Zionist Jews even in the middle of the war, as there still are anti-Zionist Jews today. Their most well-known organization, started in 1943, is called the American Council for Judaism and it 'seeks to advance the universal principles of a Judaism free of nationalism'. Its sister organization, called American Jewish Alternatives to Zionism, founded in 1968, 'applies Jewish values of justice and humanity to the Arab–Israel conflict' and 'rejects nationality attachment of Jews, particularly American Jews, to the State of Israel as self-segregating, inconsistent with American constitutional concepts of individual citizenship and separation of church and state, and as being a principal obstacle to Middle East peace'. Though both of these organizations are listed annually in the *American Jewish Year Book* (from which the language of their aims is taken), their views carry no weight with the great majority of American Jewry today, just as they carried no weight with it in 1943 and in 1968.

By 1944 the Zionists, for the first time in American history, succeeded in getting each of the major political parties to build pro-Zionist planks into their presidential campaign platforms. The Democratic one read: 'We favor the opening of Palestine to un-restricted Jewish immigration and colonization, and such a policy as to result in the establishment there of a free and democratic Jewish commonwealth'. The Republican plank was somewhat longer and self-serving:[16]

> In order to give refuge to millions of distressed Jewish men, women and children driven from their homes by tyranny, we call for the opening of Palestine to their unrestricted immigra-tion and land ownership, so that in accordance with the full intent and purpose of the Balfour Declaration of 1917 and the resolution of a Republican Congress in 1922, Palestine may be constituted as a free and democratic commonwealth.

The American political establishment had thus come a long way since 1918 and 1922, when, like the Zionist movement, it accepted Britain's and the League's formulation of a Jewish *home* in Palestine. Now, again like the Zionist movement, it had switched from the concept of a home to a commonwealth. The dictionary has nine different definitions of the word 'commonwealth', ranging from the official designation for four American states (Kentucky, Massachusetts, Pennsylvania, and Virginia), to the self-governing but not completely autonomous Commonwealth of Puerto Rico, to the loose association of independent entities that belong to the (formerly British) Commonwealth of Nations. But the one definition that most people probably have in mind when they use the word is a sovereign independent state. This is certainly what almost all Zionists meant in 1944.

Franklin Delano Roosevelt won the 1944 American presidential contest. But even then, after more than a decade of loyal Jewish electoral support for him, he continued to deceive them. For instance, in March 1944 (as reported in the *New York Times* of 10 March 1944) he authorized two Zionist leaders to announce in his name that 'when future decisions are reached full justice will be done to those who seek a Jewish national home'. Yet three weeks later (as reported in the *Times* of 3 April 1944), he told Emir Abdullah of Trans-Jordan, grandfather of the present ruler of Jordan, King Hussein, that nothing would be done with regard to Palestine without prior consultation among all the parties involved. Given the known diametric differences between the Arabs and the Jews, this could only mean that the former would have a veto over the latter's aspirations.

Not only that. During the 1945 Yalta Conference with Joseph Stalin and Winston Churchill, Roosevelt sent a destroyer to fetch Saudi Arabia's monarch, King Ibn Sa'ud, from Jidda to Cairo. At the meeting between them the king did nothing to hide his scorn for the Jews or to moderate the most extreme Arab position with regard to Palestine. Yet FDR was very impressed with Ibn Sa'ud, and in his 1 March 1945 report to a joint session of Congress he remarked: [17]

> I learned more about the whole problem, the Moslem problem, the Jewish problem, by talking with Ibn Sa'ud for five minutes [– actually he spent four hours with him and no time at all with any of the Jewish leaders of Palestine –] than I could have learned in an exchange of two or three dozen letters.

The remark obviously prompted negative reactions from American Jewish Zionists. The reaction of Christian Zionists was exemplified by Senator Edwin Johnson, a member of the American Christian Palestine Committee, who quipped that 'the choice of the desert king as expert on the Jewish question is nothing short of amazing . . . I imagine that even Fala [Roosevelt's pet dog] would be more of an expert'. Even non-Zionist Jews were stunned. Samuel Rosenman, a top White House aide to Roosevelt, characterized the remark as 'almost bordering on the ridiculous'. And Bernard Baruch said that 'despite my having been a lifelong Democrat, I would rather trust my American Jewishness in Mr [Thomas] Dewey's hands [the unsuccessful Republican nominee for President] than in Mr Roosevelt's'. [18]

Six weeks later, on 12 April 1945, Franklin Delano Roosevelt died in office, leaving a varied legacy to his bereaved countrymen. To scholars he left the debate about his true feelings, intentions, actions, and constraints regarding Jews, Arabs, Palestine, and Zionism. There will always be a question, given the tenor of his time, as to whether he could have done as much for European Jewish refugees wishing to flee to America as later Presidents were able to do for, say, the Vietnamese boat people or for Cubans who came to America to escape the regime of Fidel Castro. To the Zionists and their enemies he left the controversy surrounding the possible role of the Jews of both Palestine and America in the non-rescue of European Jewry and the extent to which they may have prevented the truth about Roosevelt's procrastinations from reaching the Jewish voter. To his successor, Harry S. Truman, he left the conclusion and aftermath of World War II, including decisions concerning how far and how fast the United States should go to help transform the Jewish national home into the Jewish commonwealth or the Jewish state.

Depending upon how one looks at things, it was now Truman's turn to become either the presidential hero or the presidential villain of the continuing Palestinian piece.

7

Twentieth-Century Zionism: from Jewish Commonwealth to Jewish State

Harry Truman is the American President on whose desk there stood the famous hand-lettered sign *The Buck Stops Here*. It stopped there constantly. Just in the four years between his accession to the presidency and Israel's creation and admission into the United Nations, he had to make some of the most momentous foreign policy decisions in the modern history of his country and of the world. He had, for example, to decide on the use of the atomic bomb in the winding down of the war against Japan. He had to deal with the nature and mission of the American military governments in Japan, Germany, and Austria. He also had to consider the survivors of the Nazi Holocaust, the rise of Communist China, the expansion of the Russian empire into Eastern and Central Europe, the rehabilitation of Western Europe, the decline and fall of the Dutch, French, and British empires, and the new balance of power in the Middle East.

As far as Palestine was concerned, the Arabs, Jews, and British had cooperated with each other against the Germans and Italians during the war. (Moshe Dayan's famous black patch resulted from his loss of an eye while fighting with allied forces against Vichy-controlled Syria.) But after the war the struggle among the three groups resumed and intensified, especially the struggle between the mandatory authorities and Palestine's Jewish community, collectively known as the Yishuv (from the Hebrew word for settlement). To their earlier demand for a state the Yishuv and its supporters abroad added the new demand that the Jewish war victims of Europe be allowed to immigrate freely into the Holy Land. In the face of ever greater opposition from the Arabs who, quite rightly, felt no responsibility for the Holocaust, Great Britain refused both demands. The Jews responded by bringing immigrants into Palestine illegally. With equal determination, the British Navy stopped as much of this illicit entry as it could. Truman 'denounced the British blockade of Palestine against ships carrying Jews', but only privately.[1] In the meantime, acts of Jewish violence against British personnel and installations increased, not only by uncontrolled groups like the Stern Gang and Menachem Begin's Irgun Zva'i Leumi (National Military Organization), but also by the Haganah, the official defense body of the Yishuv. The Palestine government retaliated with curfews, martial law, searches, and jailings, including the incarceration at times of members of the Jewish Agency Executive, the entity empowered by the mandate to liaise with the British.

As the leader of the most powerful nation in the postwar period, Truman could hardly escape knowledge of the crisis or attempts to get him involved in its solution. Only a few days after he started sitting at the President's desk, he received a letter from Secretary of State Edward R. Stettinius, Jr,[2]

offering to 'brief' me on Palestine before I might be approached by any interested parties. It was likely, he said, that efforts would soon be made by some of the Zionist leaders to obtain from me some commitments in favor of . . . unlimited Jewish immigration into Palestine and the establishment there of a Jewish state.

Stettinius was right. Immigration and statehood were precisely what the Zionists wanted. Since Truman was the new President of the United States, he was the one man on earth whose support they deemed absolutely vital. Without American pressure on Britain, and on other countries if the question came to the United Nations, they were convinced there would be no significant increase in immigration and certainly no state. And so Zionist pressure on Truman began early in his administration and it never let up. This was especially true during the last days leading to the 29 November 1947 UN General Assembly resolution which recommended the creation of a Jewish state within a partitioned Palestine.

To his colleagues and cronies Truman privately complained about this pressure many times. Public complaints were of course rarer. One of the mildest appears in his memoirs as a commentary on a letter sent to him by the venerable Zionist and Jewish Agency leader, Chaim Weizmann, just two days before the Palestine partition vote in the General Assembly. Weizmann had written in his letter:

> It is freely rumored in Washington that our people have exerted undue and excessive pressure on certain [UN] delegations . . . I cannot speak for unauthorized persons but I am in a position to assure you . . . that there is no substance in this charge as far as our representatives are concerned . . . At no time have they gone beyond the limits of legitimate and moderate persuasion.

Truman says different, however:[3]

> Unfortunately Dr Weizmann was correct only to the extent that his immediate associates were concerned. The facts were that not only were there pressure movements around the United Nations unlike anything that had been seen there before but that the White House, too, was subjected to a constant barrage. I do not think I ever had as much pressure and propaganda aimed at the White House as I had in this instance. The persistence of a few of the extreme Zionist leaders – actuated by political motives and engaging in political threats – disturbed and annoyed me.

Disturbed and annoyed as he may have been at times, Truman was a humane, fair-minded person. Within the boundaries of domestic political constraints he seemed genuinely willing to contribute to workable solutions to Palestine's intractable problems. It was not the easiest of tasks. He once wrote to one of his assistants: 'I surely wish God Almighty would give the Children of Israel an Isaiah, the Christians a St Paul, and the Sons of Ishmael a peep at the Golden Rule.'[4]

Increased and immediate Jewish immigration was a demand that Truman had no trouble accepting. Despite the Holocaust, Americans were not crying out for the admission of displaced European Jews into the United States. Quite the contrary. In 1943 78 percent of those queried told the National Opinion Research Center of the University of Chicago that admitting more immigrants into the country after the war would be 'a bad idea'. Five years later, the war won, the Elmo Roper Organization asked Americans: 'If most of these refugees should turn out to be [Germans/Jews] do you think we should put a special limit on the number of them we take in?' Fifty-three percent answered 'Yes' for the Germans; an even larger number – 60 percent – answered 'Yes' for the Jews! [5]

But aside from these numerical signals, Truman had his own personal reasons for supporting more Jewish immigration into Palestine. Simply as a human being, he was appalled by the fate of the Holocaust's survivors. As a student of history and a Bible-reading Baptist, he considered the Holocaust as much a Christian failing as it was a Jewish tragedy. More than most of his country-men, he understood why so many of the survivors would not voluntarily return to, or remain in, lands full of the stink of the concentration camp, the stench of the gas chamber, and the stare of the anti-Semite.

But the demand for the more or less immediate creation of a Jewish state was another matter altogether, and Truman's first reactions were negative. He was, after all, a new President in a new world, and he had to ask himself some questions. What about Palestinian Arab opposition, which was well known and unbending? What about America's dependence – even then – on oil from other Arab countries? They also opposed a Jewish state – indeed, even a minimally autonomous Jewish presence – in Palestine. World War II had weakened Britain's overall position in the Middle East. Would American support for a Jewish state weaken it still further? Would such support help the Russians increase their own influence in the area? Would the East European origin of so many of the Yishuv's members and of the Jewish displaced persons (DPs) make a Jewish state susceptible to communist infiltration or, even worse, communist domination? Would the American people favor the creation of a Jewish state? And, most especially, how would they react if American soldiers were needed to ensure the security of the fledgling state?

Survey research has supplied answers to some of these questions. In December 1944, and again in November 1945, Americans were asked to react to the following proposition: 'There are over a million Arabs and over half a million Jews in Palestine. Do you think the British, who control Palestine, should do what some Jews ask and set up a Jewish state there, or should they do what some Arabs ask and not set up a Jewish state?' The first time around only 36 percent favored a Jewish state. The second time around, the percentage rose to 42, six points higher, but still less than a majority.

In both surveys, when those who were not opposed to the idea of statehood were asked: 'Do you think that the United States Government should officially demand that Palestine be made into a Jewish state, or don't you think so', only 20 per cent answered 'Should'. In January 1946 the 58 percent of a sample of Americans who claimed they followed the news about the disorders in the Holy Land were asked: 'Would you approve or disapprove of sending United States soldiers to maintain peace there?' Only 7 percent said they approved. In May 1946 Americans were asked to react to this proposition:

> The report of the Anglo-American Committee recommends that 100,000 Jewish refugees be admitted to Palestine in spite of protests by the Arabs there. President Truman has said that he thinks this ought to be done . . . [If] trouble breaks out between the Jews and the Arabs . . . should [we] help keep order there, or should we keep out of it?

Sixty-one percent answered 'Keep out of it'. In that same month, when another survey specifically mentioned the phrase 'our sending troops to Palestine' to aid the British to maintain law and order, 74 percent disapproved. On the other hand, in November 1947 65 percent of the Americans sampled favored the formation of 'a United Nations volunteer army' – an army that presumably could have contained some American contingents – to handle the law and order task.[6] Such was the statistical situation when Truman was involved in the Palestine question.

In June 1945 he asked Earl G. Harrison, formerly United States Commissioner of Immigration and then dean of the University of Pennsylvania Law School, to visit Europe and report the views of the stateless and unrepatriable people there. Deliberately, neither Truman nor the State Department mentioned Palestine in their instructions to him. This is because both the President and his professional diplomats wanted to believe at the time that there was no connection between the fate of Palestine and the fate of the Jewish refugees. But Harrison's final report, submitted in August, soon disabused them of this belief. Harrison wrote:

> It is my understanding . . . that certificates for immigration to Palestine will be practically exhaused by the end of the current month. What is the future to be? To anyone who has visited

the concentration camps and who has talked with the despairing survivors, it is nothing short of calamitous to contemplate that the gates of Palestine should be soon closed.

Harrison basically agreed with the Jewish Agency's request to Britain for 100,000 additional immigration permits, and he added that 'No other single matter is . . . so important from the viewpoint of Jews in Germany and Austria and those elsewhere who have known the horrors of concentration camps as is the disposition of the Palestine question'.[7] Incidentally, Harrison's conclusion that the vast majority of Jewish displaced persons wanted to go to Palestine was confirmed by General Dwight D. Eisenhower, the American military commander in Europe, in his own letter to the President a month later. Harrison and Eisenhower thus destroyed the contention of those who believed that large numbers of Jewish DPs would have chosen to come to America if America had welcomed them there.

Truman himself called the Harrison Report 'a moving document'. No doubt he was also moved by a petition that linked Jewish immigration to a Jewish Palestine, sent to him in July by the governors of thirty-seven of the then forty-eight states, as well as by a letter from fifty-four of the ninety-six members of the Senate and 250 of the 435 members of the House, making the same linkage.[8] So on 31 August he wrote a long letter to the British Prime Minister, Clement Attlee, whose Labour Party had been strongly pro-Zionist when it was out of power, to admit 100,000 Jewish DPs into Palestine immediately, irrespective of the final disposition of the country's political problems. While waiting for Attlee's final reply, Truman was undoubtedly aware of the October speech to the Senate by James E. Murray of Montana, a state with only about 1,700 Jewish residents in 1945. Murray described Britain's role in Palestine as 'a black chapter in English history', full of 'evasion and duplicity'. For good measure, he added that 'there was hardly another interest in the memory of our generation where promises have been so lavishly made and so consistently broken'.[9]

Senator Murray spoke to the Senate midway during the period when the Americans and the British were negotiating the terms of reference of a proposed joint committee to look into and make recommendations about the refugee and immigration impasse. The greatest sticking point between the two governments was the linkage between the human future of the Jewish refugees and the political future of Jewish Palestine. The British Cabinet insisted that the word 'Palestine' be mentioned nowhere in the terms of reference; the American President insisted that it must be. Truman won. It is mentioned in three of the four terms of reference, of which the first two are the most important:[10]

1 To examine political, economic and social conditions in Palestine as they bear upon the problem of Jewish immigration and settlement therein and the well-being of the peoples now living therein.

2 To examine the position of the Jews in those countries in Europe where they have been the victims of Nazi and Fascist persecution, and the practical measures taken or contemplated to be taken in those countries to enable them to live free from discrimination and oppression and to make estimates of those who wish or will be impelled by their conditions to migrate to Palestine or other countries outside Europe.

The quid pro quo for Britain's giving in on this point was that America had to give in on another: only those recommendations agreed to by every one of the members of the commission would be considered for implementation. Foreign Secretary Ernest Bevin (whom the normally pro-British Rabbi Stephen Wise called 'an enemy of the Jewish people' and 'a foe of human justice')[11] thought he had outfoxed Truman because he could not imagine that the whole inquiry committee, including the six British members he had chosen, would come back with a unanimous report.

On 13 November 1945 Washington and London announced the creation of the Anglo-American Committee of Inquiry and on 18 December they announced the names of its members. The two co-chairmen were Joseph C. Hutcheson, a federal judge from Texas, and Sir John Singleton, a judge of Britain's High Court. The other five Americans were Frank W. Buxton, editor of the *Boston Herald*, James G. McDonald, former League of Nations High Commissioner for Refugees, Bartley C. Crum, a lawyer from San Francisco, William Phillips, a former ambassador to Italy and India, and Dr Frank Aydelotte, director of Princeton University's Institute for Advanced Studies. Their five British colleagues were Wilfrid P. Crick, economic adviser to the Midland Bank, Sir Frederic Legget, under secretary in the Ministry of Labour, Major Reginald E. Manningham-Buller, a Conservative Member of Parliament, and two Labour MPs, Lord Morrison and Richard H. S. Crossman. During February and March of 1946 the members and their staffs travelled as a group and/or as subcommittees to Germany, Poland, Czechoslovakia, Austria, Italy, Greece, Palestine, Egypt, Syria, Lebanon, Iraq, Saudi Arabia, and Trans-Jordan. From the Middle East they retired to Lausanne, Switzerland, where they thrashed out and wrote their report, which they submitted to their respective governments on 20 April 1946.

The Anglo-American Committee of Inquiry made ten recommendations. They were all agreed to unanimously, and the following five are the most significant: [12]

No. 1 We have to report that such information as we received about countries other than Palestine gave no hope of substantial assistance in finding homes for Jews wishing or impelled to leave Europe.

No. 2 We recommend (*a*) that 100,000 certificates be authorized immediately for the admission into Palestine of Jews who have been the victims of Nazi and Fascist persecution; (*b*) that these certificates be awarded as far as possible in 1946 and that actual immigration be pushed forward as rapidly as conditions will permit.

No. 3 In order to dispose, once and for all, of the exclusive claims of Jews and Arabs to Palestine, we regard it as essential that a clear statement of the following principles should be made:

I That Jew shall not dominate Arab and Arab shall not dominate Jew in Palestine. II That Palestine shall be neither a Jewish state nor an Arab state. III That the form of government ultimately to be established, shall, under international guarantees, fully protect and preserve the interests in the Holy Land of Christendom and of the Moslem and Jewish faiths.

No. 4 We have reached the conclusion that the hostility between Jews and Arabs and, in particular, the determination of each to achieve domination, if necessary by violence, make it almost certain that, now and for some time to come, any attempt to establish either an independent Palestinian State or independent Palestinian States would result in civil strife such as might threaten the peace of the world.

We therefore recommend that, until this hostility disappears, the Government of Palestine be continued as at present under mandate pending . . . a trusteeship agreement under the United Nations.

No. 7 [We] recommend that the Land Transfers Regulations of 1940 be rescinded and replaced by regulations based on a policy of freedom in the sale, lease or use of land, irrespective of race, community or creed'.

Prime Minister Attlee and Foreign Secretary Bevin were flabbergasted at the committee's unexpected unanimity, especially on the 100,000. The Zionists were pleased with the positive recommendations on immigration and land purchase but displeased with the negative ones on Jewish statehood. The Arabs, who could not accept the notion that they had to pay anything for the sins of the Europeans against the Jews, were bitter at what was essentially the suggested abrogation of the 1939 White Paper. And President Truman was both happy and hopeful. But his happiness and hope were dashed when Attlee, less than a fortnight after receiving the committee's report, announced in Parliament that the admission of the 100,000 now depended on two new conditions: the immediate disarming of 'illegal' Jewish and Arab groups in Palestine and the acceptance by the United States of a share of the 'additional military and financial responsibilities' involved in bringing the Jewish immigrants over.[13] If these new conditions were not met, Britain would continue its restrictions regardless of what the Anglo-American Committee had said and of what Britain had promised in the case of a unanimous report.

Instead of insisting that Attlee and Bevin honor their pledge to him, Truman consented to a second Anglo-American inquiry. It is usually referred to as the Morrison–Grady scheme, after Henry F. Grady, the head of the United States delegation, and Herbert Morrison, the Briton who announced it in Parliament. The Grady mission arrived in London on 12 July. By the 19th Grady was already sold on the scheme. By the 24th he was wrapping up his assignment and cabling his superiors in the State Department trying to sell it to them as well. By the 31st Morrison was announcing its details in the House of Commons.

The Morrison–Grady scheme was actually a resurrection of an

old British plan for a quasi-federalization of the Holy Land. It would have partitioned the country into a Jewish province, an Arab province, a Jerusalem district, and a district of the Negev, which is the southern half of what is today Israel. Since the British would have had defense, foreign policy, and foreign commerce control over all the districts, as well as actual local control over two of them, they were giving up no sovereignty and very little land. A group of American Senators and Congressmen noted this, somewhat passionately, when they wrote Secretary of State James F. Byrnes in the second week of August that the Morrison–Grady plan was 'a pernicious scheme to ransom the lives of displaced Hebrews by trading land for lives. In essence the British plan takes the very land required to house the displaced whose rightful territory is Palestine. The British plan invites the United States to join in creating a ghetto.' [14]

A more dispassionate analysis of the plan's deficiencies was presented to the American delegation by one of its staff members, Dr Paul L. Hanna, a non-Jew. On 21 July 1946, three days before Grady cabled his recommendation for acceptance, Hanna sent him and the other commissioners the following memorandum. It is printed here in full not only because of its coolly reasoned arguments, but also because it has never been published before.[15]

Memorandum on the Present State of the Negotiations

To: Mr Grady
        Mr Dorr
        Mr Gaston
From: Mr Hanna

The British delegation proposes to adopt a plan of provincial autonomy as the most hopeful solution of the Palestine problem and to present this plan to a conference of Arabs and Jews. In case of acceptance by this conference the plan would be put into effect under the present Mandate and the United Nations Assembly would be notified of what was being done and told that a draft trusteeship agreement embodying the new plan would be prepared for submission in 1947. It is apparently assumed that the 100,000 immigrants recommended by the Anglo-American Committee would not be issued certificates nor moved until after Arab and Jewish consent for the whole plan had been obtained. In case the plan were rejected by the

Arab-Jewish Conference and no other agreed plan emerged, the British would reserve the right to reconsider the whole matter, presumably again in consultation with the United States government. American agreement to this policy and support for it is expected.

If the utmost dispatch were employed and if Arab and Jewish consent were secured this program might be acceptable in the light of American policy.

It is almost certain, however, that both Arabs and Jews would not agree to the provincial autonomy proposal. Reluctant Jewish agreement is possible. Arab agreement is so improbable as hardly to be worthy of consideration.

What then is likely to occur under the British program? A conference of Arabs and Jews will assemble no earlier than the end of August and probably not until September or October. The Arab delegates will reject the provincial scheme and reiterate their demands for independence or will possibly express a willingness to accept a trusteeship which would provide for a mere trickle of Jewish immigration during the trusteeship and independence for an Arab Palestine within ten years. Arab violence against the provincial scheme will break out in Palestine and at other places in the Arab world. The British government will ask for new consultations with the United States and will explain that it has tried to carry out the Anglo-American agreement but cannot enforce a decision in the face of Arab opposition. It is prepared, if the United States wishes, to draft a trusteeship instrument along provincial autonomy lines and to seek agreement of the states directly concerned and, even if such agreement is not forthcoming, to submit the draft instrument in 1947 to the General Assembly. The difficulties of this proposal are so great, however, and the delay so long that the British government feels a solution should be sought in closer harmony with Arab wishes as set forth at the Arab-Jewish conference. Whatever the United States decides then and whatever the outcome of these consultations, months will have elapsed, the 100,000 Jews will not have been moved, and the White Paper Policy will have, in effect, remained in force.

Should the United States delegation accept an agreement which commits our government to support a British policy likely to have such an outcome? It seems to me that it should not. It cannot and should not try to dictate British policy in view of our unwillingness to assume responsibility or to back a policy with military force. It can and should, however, refrain from committing the United States to any joint Anglo-American policy on Palestine which might result in no action on the 100,000 immigrants, and in a final freezing of the Jewish National Home. If such a policy is to be adopted Great Britain should assume the full and sole responsibility. Our delegation should make no commitments whatsoever unless the British government agrees to admit the 100,000 Jews into Palestine regardless of the outcome of the Arab-Jewish conference and to proceed *at once* to draft for submission to the General Assembly *this* September a trusteeship instrument which would give effect either to the principle of provincial autonomy or to some solution acceptable to both Jews and Arabs if such can be found through a conference summoned for no later than August 20. This could be done either by adoption of the American definition of 'states directly concerned' or on the plea of urgency in connection with the statement that Arab rejection of the basic plan has made further negotiations pointless.

American withdrawal now from the whole Palestine affair is infinitely preferable to involvement in and moral responsibility for a policy of protracted delay and ultimately anti-Zionist outcome.

Like Hanna, Truman realized that the new scheme would delay the admission of the 100,000 Jews and maintain the 1939 White Paper restrictions. Nevertheless he was inclined to give it a try. According to Hanna, who is now emeritus professor of history and social science at the University of Florida in Gainesville, 'what really stopped a Truman–Attlee joint statement in full support of the Morrison–Grady Plan was the attitude and work in Washington of the American members of the old [that is, the first] Anglo-American Committee under prodding from [James G.] Mc-Donald'.[16] This, plus the unsuccessful British effort to sell a five-year trusteeship proposal to the Jews and the Arabs, finally forced the British in the spring of 1947 to ask for a special session of the United Nations General Assembly to make recommendations concerning the future government of Palestine.

With this new development came new challenges for the Zionists.

As the venue moved from Washington and London to New York, they staked out six main objectives. They were: (1) to get the British out of Palestine once and for all; (2) to receive UN support for a Jewish state there; (3) to convince the world, as they already had the Americans, that the issues of Palestine and the displaced European Jews were inseparable; (4) to strive for the most favorable boundaries possible in the event that partition proved the only way to get a Jewish state; (5) to secure complete control over immigration into that state; and (6) to go ahead with the state's establishment despite later suggestions to substitute a temporary UN trusteeship for the partition of the country, which the General Assembly recommended on 29 November 1947.

Once the British left Palestine and the Jews there declared their independence, in May of 1948, they sought to: (1) establish, defend, and consolidate their sovereignty; (2) prevent the diminution of the areas under their control, including the battle-won territories not originally allotted to them under the UN partition resolution; (3) obtain diplomatic recognition from as many countries as possible; and (4) have their new state admitted into the United Nations. How did the Israelis and their Zionist allies abroad fare with these objectives? More important, what role did America and Americans play in attaining them?

When the British called for the UN special Assembly session, they asked only for a committee to suggest Palestine's future status. But as soon as the session was under way, the Arab members of the United Nations tried to put a substitute item on the agenda: the immediate end of the mandate coupled with independence for all of Palestine as it was then demographically constituted. While the Jews welcomed the implicit possibilities of the British item, they feared the Arab one. Still very much a minority of the total population, they knew that making Palestine independent in 1947 or 1948 would foreclose, perhaps forever, their dream of a Jewish majority in a Jewish state. So when, with the help of the American and other UN delegations, the Arab attempt was defeated at the outset, they were relieved.

That skirmish over, the next big one concerned the composition and terms of reference of the UN investigating body. Again with the help of the American and other delegations, it was decided that none of the members of the United Nations Special Committee on Palestine (UNSCOP) would be from China, France, the United States, Russia or the United Kingdom. It was also decided that

UNSCOP would investigate conditions and talk to people in both Europe and the Middle East. UNSCOP went off to the two regions and came back to New York at the end of August 1947 with two reports. The majority report, signed by the members from Canada, Czechoslovakia, Guatemala, Holland, Peru, Sweden and Uruguay, recommended the end of British rule, the creation of economically joined but independent Arab and Jewish states, an internationalized Jerusalem area, and the admission during the transitional period of 150,000 Jewish immigrants. The minority report, signed by the Indian, Iranian, and Yugoslav members, recommended a federal state. (The Australian member refused to sign either report because neither was unanimous.)

Since even the minority report conceded merit in the concept of a Jewish homeland – the only question was its political and juridical definition – Washington was impressed with UNSCOP's work. One unnamed American official reacted with the question : 'If this doesn't constitute world public opinion, what would?' [17] But the Zionists, while delighted with the outcome so far, were still worried. On 8 October the American Christian Palestine Committee sent Truman a telegram urging him to support the majority report : [18]

> Without forthright American support the majority report will be whittled down to appease Arab and oil interests, and the Jews will be offered a ghetto instead of a state. America's declared policy on Palestine, rather than Arab threats and unwarranted economic pressures, must determine our stand on this issue.

On 11 October the American UN delegation announced its support for the majority report, a stand supported editorially by the *New York Times* the next day and by the American Federation of Labor, in convention, a few days after that.

But like all members, America has only one vote in the General Assembly. Moreover, the Assembly's rules require that a resolution can be passed only if it has the support of two-thirds of the members present and voting. So the problem from the middle of October until the end of November, when the session was scheduled to conclude, was getting that two-thirds vote in favor of partition. Everyone agreed on two points : the vote would be close, and partition had little chance without American efforts to win over wavering delegations. So our question now becomes who pressured whom to vote how?

This matter of pressure is an intriguingly difficult one to form a view on. It is a very relative and subjective term : what may appear to one person merely as an energetic expression of views may look to another like an unmitigated, undisguised attempt to coerce.

Arab spokesmen insist that the American government and the Zionists applied massive pressure upon several countries, especially in Latin America, which was then the most heavily represented geopolitical grouping in the United Nations. While probably true in some cases, this is denied by the Americans, the Zionists, and some twenty Latin American diplomats I interviewed and corresponded with thirty years ago. In fact, Dr Jorge García Granados, the Guatemalan member of UNSCOP, insists in his book *The Birth of Israel* that it was the Arabs who pressured his country and Costa Rica to take antipartition stands. Another Latin American, the chief delegate of an important country that did not vote for partition, and who was personally acquainted with the corridor tactics at the time, said in exchange for anonymity that the United States 'did not use very much pressure, if any at all. There was', he said, 'only a presentation of United States views. Even this was not very strong.' If American pressure was very strong, it is unlikely that Michael Comay, an adviser to the Jewish Agency's UN delegation at the Palestine partition session, would have written to a friend that 'a number of delegations, normally susceptible to American views, told us that they had been given to understand that Washington did not insist on their support on this particular issue'. Comay called Belgium, Holland, and Luxembourg 'doubtful to the end', and at one time he predicted 'probable defeat' for the partition plan.[20]

The closest thing to an official United States statement on pressure comes from General John Hilldring, a member of the United States delegation to the Second General Assembly. Speaking to a United Jewish Appeal meeting some weeks after the partition vote, General Hilldring said :

The United States Government took the position that every member of the United Nations, large or small, interested or disinterested, was entitled to its own independent judgement on the merits of the problem. To this policy the US Delegation subscribed whole-heartedly . . . Certainly, we tried as best we could to persuade other countries of the logic and justice of our position. I am glad that we succeeded. But we succeeded not because of threats, intimidation, or pressure indulged in by any member of the US Delegation or by any official of your government. I am sure that the cause of the new Jewish State is immeasurably more secure and that the hearts and minds of all Americans . . . will be comforted and reassured by the knowledge that its officials did not resort to sordid tactics in the Palestine dealings.

Zvi Ganin, whose book *Truman, American Jewry, and Israel, 1945–1948* is the best chronicle of the period, says that the President remained neutral 'until almost the very last day, when he yielded to Jewish pressure and instructed the US delegation to assure the attainment of the two-thirds majority'.[21] Thomas J. Hamilton, the then chief of the United Nations Bureau of the *New York Times*, says : 'It is a matter of record that there was no United States pressure until the final week before the vote'. But Hamilton adds that while America applied the greatest influence upon the UN to gain acceptance of its proposals for the setting up of a Balkan Commission, for example, 'No such comparable influence was exerted in behalf of the partition plan'.[22]

In any case, the two-thirds majority was obtained – but only barely : thirty-three in favor, thirteen against, and ten abstentions. It was so close that one may wonder how much pressure America applied. Cuba, a virtual economic colony of the United States in 1947, was the only country in the Western Hemisphere to vote against partition. Little powerless Central American countries like El Salvador and Honduras abstained. And Greece and Turkey, dependent upon American political, military, and economic aid under the Truman Doctrine, also voted against partition and a Jewish state.

In general, the Jews of Palestine and of the Diaspora were ready to accept a truncated state. But their next problem was to keep the United States and United Nations faithful to the commitment made to them on 29 November 1947. This was not easy. First of all, in December the British announced their intention to leave Palestine in May, no matter what happened. Secondly, while countries far away from the Middle East could see the justice of partitioning Palestine, the Arabs could not, and they bitterly resented any assertions that they should. So violence between the Jews and

Arabs of Palestine increased dramatically, as did incursions into Palestine by armed Arabs living in the surrounding countries. The massive breakdown of law and order frightened Truman and emboldened those in the State Department and the Defense Department (especially Defense Secretary James V. Forrestal), who had opposed partition from the very beginning. Not only did these revisionists talk Truman into announcing that no American troops would be sent to Palestine (an announcement most Americans did not mind), but they also talked him into imposing an American arms embargo to the Middle East (which many Americans, including Senators Warren G. Magnuson of Washington state, Owen Brewster of Maine, and Francis J. Myers of Pennsylvania, very much minded). If strictly enforced, the embargo had to hurt the Jews more than the Arabs, and it did. (In fact, much of the relatively little armament the Israelis got from abroad came from Eastern Europe.) But most important of all, the antipartitionists in Truman's administration tried to accomplish a complete American volte-face on partition.

On 19 March 1948, without, Truman claims, his prior knowledge and approval, the American representative on the Security Council suddenly stated that because of the internal violence and the foreign incursions,[23]

> my government believes that a temporary trusteeship for Palestine should be established under the Trusteeship Council of the United Nations to maintain the peace and afford the Jews and Arabs of Palestine, who must live together, further opportunity to reach an agreement regarding the future government of that country . . . Pending the meeting of the special session of the General Assembly, we believe that the Security Council should instruct the Palestine Commission to suspend its efforts to implement the proposed partition plan.

The *New York Times*, in its 21 March 1948 editorial, called the reversal 'a plain and unmistakable surrender to the threat of force', adding that American policy on Palestine 'has seldom been matched for ineptness in the handling of any international issue by an American administration'. Truman was embarrassed. His press secretary, Charlie Ross, wrote in his notes that the pronouncement had placed the President 'in the most embarrassing position of his political career' and he quotes Truman as telling him that the State

Department has 'made me out a liar and a doublecrosser!'[24] The Zionists were furious. Many Christians, both in and out of politics, were outraged. And many foreign diplomats at the United Nations were dismayed. Here are the reactions of just two of them.[25]

1 First they [that is, the Americans] convinced us that partition was the only answer. Now they are trying to convince us that partition is insane. It is true that I represent a small nation that cannot stand alone. I am willing to accept United States leadership. But this is treachery. By this latest reversal the United States has forfeited whatever moral justification it once had for leading the small nations.

2 . . . any form of trusteeship was 'temporary' by definition; but if . . . it was a question of waiting until the Arabs and the Jews reached agreement, the trusteeship might well last for centuries.

In the end the American proposal came to naught. Actually, it never had a real beginning, for it was not brought to a vote. This was so, in the words of the State Department publication *United States Participation in the United Nations: Report by the President to the Congress for the Year 1948*, because it soon 'became evident that the necessary two-thirds majority of delegations present and voting could not be mustered in support of a temporary trusteeship for Palestine'. Even if the necessary majority had been mustered, it would have been pointless. The British were still adhering to their intention to leave Palestine on 15 May 1948 and the Jews to theirs to proclaim an independent state as soon as the British left.

The more apparent it became that the Yishuv would do what it had promised to do, the more pressure Truman faced to recognize the emerging state. A few days before the British were scheduled to leave Palestine, Bartley C. Crum, a member of the 1946 Anglo-American Committee of Inquiry, Henry A. Atkinson, secretary of the Church Peace Union, Leon Henderson, chairman of the Americans for Democratic Action, Freda Kirchway, editor of *The Nation*, Philip Murray, the labor leader who was president of the Congress of Industrial Organizations (CIO), James G. Patton, president of the Farmers' Educational and Cooperative Union, and T. O. Thackery, editor and publisher of the *New York Post*, signed an open letter urging Truman to recognize the new state. In addition, they asked for American economic aid, an arms embargo to the countries of the Arab League, American military aid to the

Haganah, the Jewish Agency's 'army', and a UN Security Council resolution condemning Arab aggression in Palestine as a threat to world peace. Senators and Congressmen also peppered the President with similar appeals.

Besides these pressures, Truman had other considerations on his mind: his own innate humaneness, his earlier propartition statements, his personal promise to support Israel and its enlarged territorial integrity, which he gave to Dr Chaim Weizmann at the behest of Eddie Jacobson, his closest Jewish friend and World War I buddy, the coming 1948 general election (with its need for Jewish votes and campaign contributions), his bitterness at the State Department, and his concern for United Nations prestige, and finally, the plain 'force of the newly emerging reality in Palestine'.[26] The cumulative effect of all these pressures and considerations led Truman on 14 May 1948 – at 6.11 p.m. Washington time and 12.11 a.m. Jerusalem time – to issue the following announcement.[27]

> This Government has been informed that a Jewish state has been proclaimed in Palestine, and recognition has been requested by the provisional government thereof.
>
> The United States recognizes the provisional government as the *de facto* authority of the new State of Israel.

Under Truman, America became the first great power and the first nation in the world to recognize the sovereign Jewish polity, an act which encouraged many other states to do the same within the next days and months. On 31 January 1949 he extended *de jure* recognition and on 11 May 1949 his delegation joined with other countries in making Israel the fifty-ninth member of the United Nations. Zvi Ganin has called Harry Truman the 'midwife of the State of Israel'.[28] It is doubtful, however, that he would have felt politically able to bring the new baby into the world if he had not correctly perceived the changes in his countrymen's attitudes toward Jews and Jewish aspirations. As Charles Herbert Stember and his associates have put it:[29]

> Though wary of possible involvement, Americans, by and large, favored a Jewish state; and soon after Israel came into existence, they began to view her as a useful ally. Throughout, most of the American people refused to condemn the Jews [including those who were their fellow citizens] for their

efforts to create a nation of their own. On the contrary, a large portion of the public thought the long record of persecution and the unsolved [Jewish] refugee problem entitled them to a permanent homeland.

But were these the only reasons why the American public favored its government's support of Palestine's partition in order to achieve a Jewish state? Or were they also worried that without partition there might have been unbearable pressure for big, prosperous, and relatively empty America to admit the Jewish survivors of Hitler's Holocaust if Palestine remained closed to them? Only five days before the partition vote, the Palestine Committee of the Second General Assembly narrowly voted down a suggestion that the United Nations recommend refugee quotas to each of the member states. What would have happened if that resolution, rather than the partition resolution, had been taken and passed in the Assembly?

But history decided otherwise. As a result, twenty centuries of Jewish dreams, three centuries of America–Old Testament–Israel interaction, and half a century of Zionist political activity had come to a fruitful conclusion.

Part Two

Essays on the Present and the Future

8

Jewish Lobby, Jewish Vote

On 21 August 1979 James McDonough, a columnist for the *San Juan Star*, wrote that Puerto Ricans on the island ought to use the Puerto Rican community on the mainland 'in the service of the patria'. He added that Puerto Ricans in both places

> are truly amazed at the enormous success of Israel to rally Jewish support within the United States in defense of Israeli interests. The mayor of New York and senators of the state of New York are ardent supporters of Israel precisely because they owe their positions to the New York Jewish vote. Newspapers, books, films, television are all rallied to generally defend Israel and to support the idea of a special relationship between the United States and Israel.

Part of McDonough's assumptions are correct. Israel and its organized supporters in the United States have been enormously successful in rallying American Jews to the defense of that country, and most Americans do seem to accept the idea of a special relationship between the United States and Israel, just as they accept it between the United States and the United Kingdom. But how correct are some of his other assumptions, which appear to be widely held, especially abroad? Is the Jewish vote nationwide, and even in New York, really that crucial to the outcome of presidential and congressional elections today? Can an admittedly well-organized ethnic community, which makes up less than 3 percent of the total American population and which has the most rapidly declining birthrate in the United States, really force the other 97 percent to allow the American government to adopt policies and positions against its will and better judgment? In short, is the so-called Jewish or Zionist lobby in the United States, both by vote and voice, really as powerful and all-winning as it, its friends, and its enemies believe? Before we can answer any of these questions, we must first know something about the institutionalization and operation of American Jewry.

If you look at the 'National Jewish Organizations' section of the 1980 *American Jewish Year Book* and omit specialized and often very large subdivisions of individual organizations, you find that the number of these national groups approaches 300. If you add to that figure some 230 local federations, welfare funds, and community relations councils – but not America's 5,000 synagogues and temples – you reach a total of 500 Jewish organizations engaged in interest group articulation, much of it concerned with Israel's problems and fate. Others might single out different organizations, but in my judgment the three most influential ones are the National Jewish Community Relations Advisory Council (popularly known by its initials, NJCRAC), the Conference of Presidents of Major American Jewish Organizations (referred to within the Jewish community as the Presidents' Conference), and AIPAC, the American Israel Public Affairs Committee. NJCRAC derives its influence from the fact that it is an umbrella organization representing 102 local Jewish agencies and eleven national ones: the American Jewish Committee, American Jewish Congress, B'nai B'rith and its Anti-Defamation League, Hadassah, Jewish Labor Committee, Jewish War Veterans of the USA, National Council of Jewish Women, Union of American Hebrew Congregations, Union of Orthodox Jewish Congregations of America, United Synagogue of America, and Women's American ORT (Organization for Rehabilitation through Training). Its 1980 national plenum in Philadelphia was addressed by the following political, government, and other officials in this order, as listed in the program: Wilson Goode, the managing director of the city of Philadelphia; David Aaron, the deputy assistant to the President for national security affairs; Shmuel Tamir, Israel's Minister of Justice; Robert W. Farrand, the officer-in-charge of bilateral relations of the Soviet desk of the Department of State; Rachamin Alazar, the representative of the Association of Ethiopian Jews in Israel; Stuart E. Eisenstat, President Carter's assistant for domestic affairs and policy; Ohio Democratic Senator, Howard Metzenbaum; Benjamin Hooks, executive director of the National Association for the Advancement of Colored People; William Green, the mayor of Philadelphia; Ephraim Evron, the Israeli ambassador to the United States; and the labor leader Lane Kirkland, who succeeded the late, very pro-Israel, George Meany as president of the very pro-Israel AFL-CIO.

To take just one example from this list of speakers, it is both impressive and instructive that David Aaron (who as deputy to President Carter's national security adviser, Dr Zbigniew Brzezinski, was a very busy man worrying about all regions of the world) spent the greater part of a day talking about and listening to the concerns about Israel of the delegates to the NJCRAC convention.

As for the Conference of Presidents of Major American Jewish Organizations, its influence flows from the fact that, once its constituent bodies agree on an issue, a statement, or an action, it can speak and act for thirty-five national organizations, one of which – the Council of Jewish Federations and Welfare Funds – is an observer. Subtracting those organizations that belong to both the NJCRAC and the Presidents' Conference, the latter's affiliated organizations are the American Israel Public Affairs Committee, American Mizrachi Women, American Zionist Federation, B'nai B'rith Women, Bnai Zion, Central Conference of American Rabbis, Emunah Women of America, Jewish National Fund, Jewish Reconstructionist Foundation, Labor Zionist Alliance, Mizrachi-Hapoel Hamizrachi, National Committee for Labor Israel, National Council of Young Israel, National Federation of Temple Sisterhoods, National Jewish Community Relations Advisory Council, National Jewish Welfare Board, North American Jewish Youth Council, Pioneer Women, Rabbinical Assembly, Rabbinical Council of America, Women's League for Conservative Judaism, World Zionist Organization – American Section, and the Zionist Organization of America.

It is remarkable that the Presidents' Conference has so much stature – in its own eyes, in the eyes of the media who report on it, and in the eyes of foreign and domestic diplomats and politicians who meet with it.[1] Here are some random examples. On 1 April 1976 Rabbi Alexander M. Schindler, the then ex-chairman of the Conference, held a press conference in Tel-Aviv as part of an official visit to Israel at the invitation of Labor Prime Minister Yitzchak Rabin. On 18 March 1976 a delegation from the Conference travelled to Washington to meet with French President Valéry Giscard d'Estaing and with Jacques Koscuisko-Morizet, the French ambassador to the United States. In their *Annual Report* the leaders of the Conference made clear their conviction that

the French President had invited the delegation as part of his effort to improve the French image in America and to overcome the legacy of the [Charles] de Gaulle era, a legacy that had created for France a reputation for anti-Americanism. At the meeting, President Giscard d'Estaing, expressing high esteem for the French Jewish community [the largest in Western Europe], underlined with great pride his country's vote at the UN General Assembly the previous November opposing the 'Zionism is racism' resolution.

With regard to that 1975 UN resolution which equated Zionism with racism and with South African-type apartheid, on the eve of the Jewish High Holy Days and of the Thirty-First General Assembly the Presidents' Conference UN Task Force sent letters to eighty-five UN delegations. Eighteen of the representatives of key nations that had voted for the resolution were asked to 'oppose vigorously all efforts that would, directly or indirectly, malign and assault the Jewish people'. Thirty-three ambassadors who had opposed the resolution were asked to oppose any similar efforts at future UN sessions. Thirty-four of the ambassadors who had either absented themselves or abstained from voting were reminded in rather rabbinic rhetoric that 'abstention or absence when the issue is profoundly moral, only contributes to strengthening the forces of darkness'. In addition, thirty-seven ambassadors from Asian and black African countries were urged not to tie Zionism to apartheid, especially during the UN's so-called Decade Against Racism.

On 19 October 1976 Israel's UN ambassador, Chaim Herzog, and his American counterpart, William W. Scranton, addressed a meeting of the Conference of Presidents that was well covered by the media. Ambassador Scranton said that the United States was 'determined' to fight the Zionism-is-racism-or-apartheid equation because 'it's wrong, absolutely wrong, and we will not allow it'. At that same meeting the Israeli delegate charged that the United Nations Secretariat was being 'Arabized' and was becoming a 'world center of anti-Semitism'. On the matter of linking Zionism to South Africa's racial policies because of Israel's tiny (two-fifths of 1 percent) trade with that country, Ambassador Herzog threatened to publicize, in the words of the Presidents' Conference *Report*, 'a full and documented account of the extensive and far greater trade by other UN members, including Arabs and Africans, with South Africa's regime'.

The Conference of Presidents of Major American Jewish Organizations even took on the government of Mexico. At a time when both Jews and non-Jews the world over were rejoicing at Israel's successful rescue of the hostages at the airport in Entebbe, Uganda, Mexican President Luís Echeverría ordered his UN ambassador to condemn the raid in a letter to the Security Council. After a perfunctory condemnation of 'all terrorist acts', the ambassador wrote that:

> Mexico, faithful to its principles, cannot likewise fail to express its firm rejection of the use of armed force by any State as a means of trying to solve conflicts, because such acts are a flagrant violation both of the Charter of the United Nations and of universally accepted principles of international law, and create precedents of incalculable danger for all civilized coexistence.

The American Jewish community and the Presidents' Conference were so enraged at Mexico's Zionism-equals-racism vote and at the letter from the Mexican ambassador that individual Jews and those Jewish organizations which sponsor tours to Mexico through their travel departments stopped going there for their vacations and holidays. Mexico's tourist industry suffered terribly as a result. Only after it was learned that Mexico's actions were dictated by President Echeverría's unsuccessful bid to become the next Secretary-General of the United Nations (a bid that would have required Soviet and Third World support) did the American Jewish community reduce and then end its boycott of Mexico. In November 1976 six American Jewish leaders were among the foreign guests invited to attend the inauguration of the new Mexican President, José López Portillo. Seymour Graubard of the Anti-Defamation League, who had earlier led a Presidents' Conference delegation to meet with President Echeverría in 1975, now announced that Mexico's voting patterns at the United Nations were 'a cause for optimism', and the Israel-related Mexico–American Jewish storm blew away.

When Secretary of State Henry A. Kissinger left his post after the election of Jimmy Carter, the Presidents' Conference hosted a public luncheon for him. Two of his remarks stand out. The first was:

> From my point of view, probably no criticism has hurt me more than if it came from this community: probably, from your point of view, it was especially painful if disagreements

occurred between the Jewish community and the first Jewish Secretary of State in American history.

(Note that Kissinger equated the Presidents' Conference with the American Jewish community.) His second remark was :

I thought it was important for the future of Israel and for the future of the Jewish people that the actions the United States government took were not seen to be the result of a special personal relationship, that the support we gave Israel reflected . . . the basic national interest of the United States, transcending the action of who might be in office at any particular period.

Prime Minister Menachem Begin of Israel and President Jimmy Carter of the United States came to power in the same year, 1977, and the Conference of Presidents of Major American Jewish Organizations wooed and were wooed by both men in both countries. In May 1977 the chairman and executive director of the Presidents' Conference went off to Jerusalem at the invitation of Begin. Upon their return, they met first with the Undersecretary of State for Political Affairs and the Assistant Secretary of State for Middle Eastern Affairs. Immediately afterwards, they met with presidential aides Robert Lipshutz and Stuart Eizenstat at the White House to complain about the apparent 'erosion' of President Carter's 'commitment to Israel'. On 10 June 1977 the *New York Times* reported that the President was 'stung' by the criticism and was going to take steps to 'repair the relationship'. On 6 July he did indeed confer with more than fifty Jewish leaders in the Cabinet Room of the White House, a conference witnessed in part by the news media.

Even the late President Anwar al-Sadat acknowledged the importance – it makes no difference whether the importance is real or perceived – of the Presidents' Conference. In mid-January of 1978 he met with the chairman and the executive director of the Conference at Aswan. Besides talking with Sadat, the two Jewish leaders from America spent six days in Egypt exchanging views with the then Vice-President Hosni Mubarak, National Assembly Speaker Sayyed Marei, Minister of State Butros Ghali, and other Egyptian government officials, businessmen, industrialists, professors, and journalists.

There is another aspect of the work of the Presidents' Conference that has to be mentioned : its service as the public relations role model for its constituent organizations and for their constituents, as well as for others. The Conference *Report* for the fiscal year ending 31 March 1978 contains a letter, which is reprinted here because it is a prime illustration of how non-Jewish support for Israel is mobilized on both national and local levels :

The swiftly-changing Middle East scene is moving into a new and crucial period, one that demands vigorous and informed action by an alert and vigilant Jewish community. How clearly these events are understood by the American people and the makers of public policy is likely to determine both the future of the Jewish State and the chances of peace in the Middle East.

(1) Through political action and public education we must make clear that there can be no peace if the murderous band of terrorists who call themselves the Palestine Liberation Organization are permitted to take part in the Geneva peace talks. By word and deed – by its charter and by its frightful acts of violence – the PLO has disqualified itself from any table at which the peaceful settlement of disputes is discussed.

(2) Through political action and public education we must make clear that there can be no peace in the Middle East, no security for America's ally Israel and no protection for American interests in the creation of a so-called Palestinian state. By its very existence, such a state would offer a base for terrorist incursion and Soviet political intrusion of the Middle East, thus exploding whatever settlement is reached by Israel and the Arab states.

(3) Through political action and public education we must make clear that there can be no peace unless it is a negotiated peace, agreed to in treaties signed by the parties, and that neither the United States nor the Soviet Union – separately or acting in concert – can set the terms of the negotiations or determine their outcome.

(4) Through political action and public education we must make clear that there can be no peace if it is based on the joint US Soviet declaration of October 1, 1977. Productive negotiations at Geneva can be based only on UN Resolution 242, which calls for a 'just settlement of the refugee problem' and which affirms the 'sovereignty, territorial integrity and political independence of every state in the area' living within 'secure and recognized boundaries'.

In interpreting these vital issues to our fellow Americans, we will be serving the interests of our country and the cause of Middle East peace – and thus the security and dignity of our fellow Jews abroad.

In sum, as far as American domestic politics are concerned, the Presidents' Conference believes that it plays a role, especially during presidential election years. There is truth in this belief.

The third Jewish organization of special significance is AIPAC – the American Israel Public Affairs Committee. It is unique in two ways. First, whereas all the other organizations mentioned are tax-exempt and live on contributions that are also tax-exempt, AIPAC admits to being, and advertises itself as, a legally registered domestic lobbying organization on behalf of a foreign government and claims that therefore all contributions to it by Americans are *not* tax-exempt. Secondly, unlike other domestic lobbying organizations for other foreign governments, AIPAC has never charged Israel for its services. Instead, all of its money is raised by appeals to friendly individuals and groups in the United States.

Its status and its idealism with regard to the way it gets its money is both a curse and a blessing. The curse is that its coffers are never full enough and its staff is never large enough. The blessing is that, free from the restrictions which the Internal Revenue Service imposes on all tax-exempt organizations, AIPAC can do and say things, especially to important elected and appointed officials at the White House, the State Department, the Pentagon, and on Capitol Hill, where the House and Senate and their staffs sit, that no other pro-Israel tax-exempt group can. No wonder that the *Washington Post* has called it 'a power to be reckoned with at the White House, State and Defense Departments and on Capitol Hill' and the *New York Times* has called it 'the most powerful, best-run and effective foreign policy interest group in Washington'.[2] No wonder, too, that in one of its promotional brochures AIPAC proudly proclaims: 'Since the 1973 [Syrian–Egyptian–Israeli] War, Congress has approved more than $11 billion in aid to Israel – almost $1 billion more than requested by three [presidential] Administrations'.[3]

I doubt that this foreign aid feat was achieved by AIPAC's efforts alone, but apparently it does not mind if others draw that conclusion. I also doubt that American Jewry all by itself has ever had the clout to force the American government to take any position in the Arab-Israel question that it did not want to take. After all, no

American President has recognized any part of Jerusalem as Israel's capital: the American embassy has always been in Tel-Aviv. No American President has recognized the annexation of the formerly Jordanian-controlled Arab portion of Jerusalem. No American President has recognized *de jure* the Israeli occupation of the Jordanian West Bank, of the formerly Egyptian-controlled Gaza Strip, and of Syria's Golan Heights. The legality of Israeli civilian settlement in any of these areas has never been recognized by any of the American administrations in power after the 1967 war. And perhaps most instructive of all, no amount of pressure by the so-called Jewish and Zionist lobby was strong enough to prevent President Carter from agreeing to sell advanced F-15 fighters to Saudi Arabia, or to prevent President Ronald Reagan from scrapping Carter's promise not to sell it detachable fuel tanks and Sidewinder air-to-air missiles which will increase both the firepower and the range of the F-15s. Despite a bruising battle in the Senate, which ended on 20 October 1981, the so-called Jewish and Zionist lobby was clearly not strong enough to block the sale to Saudi Arabia of AWACS (Airborne Warning and Control System) planes, which can spot aircraft between approximately 200 and 400 miles away.

No one has better echoed my position on the lobby than Hyman Bookbinder, the veteran Washington representative of the American Jewish Committee. He once said it is 'idiotic to deny that there are powerful American Jews. But it doesn't add up to power for Jews *as* Jews . . . [As] for Jewish political power – large P Partisan power – there is relatively little organized Jewish political power'.[4] In other words, it is at best an oversimplification and at worst an untruth to claim or believe that American Jews control or determine what the American government wants and does in the Middle East. The best that American Jewry can do with regard to Israel is to argue its case in the public arena in the hope that non-Jewish Americans will agree that much of it is in fact consistent with the general foreign policy goals of the United States. When American Jews are able to make their case, they 'win'; when they are not able to make it, they 'lose'.

I believe there is the same kind of confusion and lack of sophistication about the so-called Jewish vote in America – even in the *New York Times*, which in an article on 8 September 1980 wrote that 'Jewish voters could be decisive, for example, in New York, Pennsylvania and Florida, states that Mr Carter carried in 1976 and most likely would have to win again to defeat Mr Reagan'. In the fall 1980 issue of *Inside*, the magazine of the *Philadelphia Jewish Exponent*, Wolf Blitzer, the Washington correspondent of the *Jerusalem Post*, made the same point : 'There is no longer any doubt that all three candidates are going after the Jewish vote. In a close race, it could be decisive.'

It is true that American Jews have one of the highest voting rates in proportion to population of any identifiable racial, religious, and ethnic group in the country. It is equally true that in the past they have given overwhelming support to candidates carrying the Democratic banner. The Jewish vote for the Democratic presidential nominee has been as high as 91 percent for Roosevelt in 1944 and as low as 65 percent for George McGovern in 1972. It is also true that, as of the 1970 national census (the one which determined the number of votes of each state in the Electoral College for the 1980 election), the Jews have tended to live in the twelve Northern and Midwest states that possessed almost half of the 538 Electoral College votes in 1980 and in many prior presidential election years. But Americans, including the Jews, are moving south and west – from the snowbelt to the sunbelt. Thus what happened in the past, both as to the distribution of Electoral College votes among the states and the way people will vote within the states, can no longer serve as a useful guide for the future.

Consider : in the 1960 contest between John F. Kennedy and Richard M. Nixon some 68 million people voted for the Democratic and Republican nominees. Yet the contest was decided in favor of Democrat Kennedy by 119,000 votes.

Consider : in the 1968 contest between Nixon and Hubert H. Humphrey some 63 million people voted for the Democratic and Republican nominees. Yet that contest was decided in favor of Republican Nixon by 510,000 votes.

Consider : in the 1976 contest between Ford and Carter about 80 million people voted for the Democratic and Republican nominees. Yet that election was decided in favor of Democrat Carter by 1,683,000 votes.

If the electoral fate of three of the five American Presidents who ran between 1960 and 1976 was decided by such small – one might say tiny – majorities, then in close elections every single person's vote can be decisive. Most people know that almost one-third of America's Jews live in New York State, and that is important because New York's forty-one Electoral College votes in 1980 were exceeded only by California's forty-five. But how many people know that New York's biggest voting bloc – if one can still use that phrase in individualistic, ticket-splitting, party-switching, politically fragmented America – are not the Jews, but the Italian–Americans? In the 1980 New York Republican primary for Senator, the winner was not the respected, long-serving Jewish Senator, Jacob K. Javits. He was Alfonse M. D'Amato, a nationally unknown Italian-American from Long Island. Later, in the general elections that year, D'Amato won a seat in the Senate and Ronald Reagan won the presidency. But as far as the latter race was concerned, according to results gathered by the American Broadcasting Company, only 42 percent of Jews voting nationally voted for Democrat Jimmy Carter and only 37 percent did so in New York State. My point is this. If Jimmy Carter, or Ronald Reagan, or John Anderson needed Jewish votes to win New York's Electoral College votes in the 1980 election, they needed Italian votes, black votes, Catholic votes, women's votes, Puerto Rican votes, and other votes just as much. And when they campaigned, they had to consider, and articulate, and make promises about the particularistic concerns of *all* these groups, not just the Jews.

Another point to consider in the Electoral College equation is the percentage of the Jewish population in the states with the highest number of votes in the College. As of the 1970 census and the 1980 elections, here are the Electoral College votes and the percentage of Jews respectively for the twelve key states : California, 45 and 3·1; New York, 41 and 12·1; Pennsylvania, 27 and 3·6; New Jersey, 17 and 6·0; Illinois, 26 and 2·4; Florida, 17 and 5·1; Massachusetts, 14 and 4·3; Maryland, 10 and 4·5; Ohio, 25 and 1·4; Connecticut, 8 and 3·3; Michigan, 21 and 1·0; and Missouri, 12 and 1·5. Except in New York, the Jewish percentage is extremely low. Nowadays, if 1 percent of the population of a state is important so is the other 99; if 12 percent is important, so is the other 88.

The argument may be put another way, a way that shows a distinct disparity between how Jews vote and their success in achieving Jewish or pro-Israel political objectives purely as a result of their voting record or perceived voting power. In 1944, by which year the horrors of the Holocaust were becoming more and more known to the outside world, American Jews gave 91 percent of their presidential vote to Franklin Delano Roosevelt. As I have shown in an earlier chapter, they elected him in full knowledge of what he failed to do for the Jews of Europe or of Palestine. In 1948 72 percent of New York's Jewish vote went to Harry Truman, who had supported the Palestine partition resolution and had recognized the new State of Israel. Nevertheless, though he won the national election, he lost New York to his Republican rival, Thomas E. Dewey. In 1973 Richard Nixon, supposedly a vindictive man, aware that fewer than one-third of the nation's Jews had voted for him the year before and that the American Constitution forbade his running for a third term no matter how the Jews might vote again, ordered an around-the-clock military resupply of Israel after it was caught off guard by the Syrians and the Egyptians in the Yom Kippur War. While we do not know all of Nixon's reasons for saving Israel, we know that they could not have been generated by gratitude for Jewish votes for him in the past or by hopes of gaining votes in a future election that he could never run in.

From all this the following conclusions can be drawn. One, no single Jewish organization or group of organizations can deliver so-called Jewish votes to a candidate just because the leaders of these organizations personally favor the candidate. In the 1940s the towering leader of American Zionism was Rabbi Abba Hillel Silver, a rabid Republican, and a close friend of Senator Robert Taft, Harry Truman's potential presidential rival in the 1946 election. Yet Silver's Republicanism did not move the Jews to forsake their loyalty to the Democratic Party, nor did it push Truman to an anti-Zionist and anti-Israel stance. Two, the automatic affinity of the Jews toward the Democratic Party is weakening, just as it is in the other ethnic groups in America. Three, the belief that fewer than 6 million Jews, no matter how cohesively they vote, how well they are organized, and how effectively they lobby, can force the United States President, Congress, and non-Jewish public to take a generally pro-Israel line because the Jews want them to is ludicrous.

What is not ludicrous – what in fact lies at the heart of the matter – is an anecdote often told by Professor John Roche. Roche is an American Christian of Irish descent who is more Zionist than most Jews and some Israelis. For a time he was an aide to Lyndon B. Johnson, when the latter was President. At the 1967 meeting between Johnson and Soviet Premier Alexei Kosygin in Glassboro, New Jersey, Kosygin, writes Roche, 'asked President Johnson quite clinically – like a doctor exploring a quaint eccentricity – why we supported Israel against the Arab world with all its resources. LBJ replied simply "Because we think it's right".' [5] That belief – nothing more and nothing less – is the real power behind the Jewish lobby and the Jewish vote in America.

9

The Economics of Israeli Existence

The Jews of Palestine and later of Israel have always been dependent on funds from abroad. This has been true no matter how many economic sacrifices they have made. But it became truer with the creation of the state and the resulting costs of immigration, absorption, development, and defense. These costs have skewed the Israeli economy and created some interesting facts and figures.[1]

As of the fall of 1980, Israel's annualized inflation rate was 134 percent. In the preceding twelve months food prices rose by 169·5 percent; clothing by 96·5 percent; education, entertainment, and culture by 115 percent; and medical care by 141·4 percent. Israelis pay perhaps the highest tax rates in the world. They have the highest foreign debt in the world. It was $19·2 billion in 1980, which was $4·2 billion more than their entire gross national product for that year. Israelis also have the highest per capita foreign debt in the world : about $5,000 a year for every man, woman, and child in the country. Defense and security took about 15 percent of the GNP and about 30 percent of the government budget in 1980. In addition to all of these nonvoluntary assaults on the gross pay of the average Israeli, there are constant pressures for voluntary monetary contributions, especially to Zahal (the Hebrew acronym for IDF, or the Israeli Defense Forces), as illustrated by the plea to the 'Citizens of Israel' on page 108.

Because Israel's own fiscal resources are insufficient, it has had to go to friendly governments and individuals for aid. Most of the friendly foreign individuals have been American Jews and the most friendly government has been the United States. This was foreseen as far back as 1921. Dr Arthur Ruppin, head of the Zionists' settlement department, said then : 'To make the national home for the Jews in Palestine a success depends upon their brethren in America . . . Zionism will not die if America does not send money to Palestine . . . but it will delay the development of the country'.[2] Here are some examples of his brethren's efforts.

In 1924 the Palestine Foundation Fund announced that during the preceding three years 70,000 American Jews had donated $6 million dollars to the organization. In 1926 the Jewish National Fund, the still-existing Zionist land-purchasing and reforesting agency, announced that Americans had contributed $500,000 more to the JNF than in the previous year. The money came in small amounts, probably for the most part from the little blue-and-white boxes that many Eastern European immigrant Jews used to keep in their kitchens. The boxes had locks which could only be opened at the JNF's offices. Many a Jewish mother and grand-mother used to joyfully turn over her filled box in the hope that

Source: Jerusalem Post International Edition, 21–7 September 1980, p. 7.

her meager contribution would help *'zu boiyen a yiddishe medineh in Palestineh'* ('to build a Jewish state in Palestine').

In 1928 the president of the Zionist Organization of America reported that contributions to the cause in 1927 were again $500,000 more than they had been in the previous year. By the end of 1928 the Zionist movement worldwide had put $18 million into Palestine; 60 percent of it came from America. In 1930 the Palestine National Loan Fund announced that between October 1929 and March 1930 – during the height of the Stock Market Crash – it had collected over $300,000, almost three times more than during the same period the year before. The 25 May 1939 edition of the United States *Congressional Record* (p. 6167) notes that by that year 'Americans have invested over $100,000,000 in Palestine'.

The principal organization for collecting voluntary donations from Americans and sending them on to Israel is the United Jewish Appeal. The UJA was established in January 1939 through a merger of three organizations. One of them, the United Israel Appeal, still exists and has existed since 1925. Originally called the United Palestine Appeal, UIA receives money from the UJA and channels it to Israel, where it is used for

> a full range of services and programs – language and vocational training, housing, social welfare, rural settlement, youth care and support for pre-school and higher education – all stemming from its primary concern for the movement, reception and absorption of immigrants from every corner of the earth.[3]

From 1948 until the end of 1979, UIA sent Israel a total of $3.453 billion. This figure does not include an additional $275 million spent in Israel during the same period by the Joint Distribution Committee, another of the UJA's 'partners', which specializes in rescue, relief and rehabilitation.[4]

Nor does it include an astronomical sum which Israel's late Prime Minister, Golda Meir, raised in a short time for the secret purchase of arms in Europe (mostly from Russia and Czechoslovakia) during the months of waning British rule in Palestine. The need for arms (which the American government of the day would not supply) was so acute that David Ben-Gurion himself was prepared to drop everything and rush to the United States to appeal to his Jewish brethren for a hoped-for $10 to $25 million. Golda Meir (then known as Golda Myerson) persuaded Ben-Gurion that she should go in his place. She arrived in the United States in January 1948 and her first appearance was in Chicago, on the 21st, before the General Assembly of the Council of Jewish Federations and Welfare Funds, an organization that at the time could be described only as 'non-Zionist'. When 'our Golda' – as American Jews are fond of calling her because she was raised in Milwaukee, Wisconsin, before she emigrated to Palestine – finished speaking, these non-Zionists in one afternoon pledged $25 million to the Palestinian Jewish struggle. In the ensuing weeks she raised another $25 million from speeches all over America.

Twenty-five years later Golda Meir wrote about how moved she was by these acts of generosity. Regarding the response to her Chicago speech, she says in her autobiography : 'They listened, and they wept, and they pledged money in amounts that no community had ever given before'.[5] When she later appeared at an elegant affair in Palm Beach, Florida, she was momentarily taken aback at the jewels and the furs and other evidences of her audience's wealth. She thought to herself : 'These people don't want to hear about fighting and death in Palestine.'[6] But she was wrong, because by the time the evening was over, these people of jewels and furs and wealth had pledged $1·5 million. Of her entire American tour she writes : 'I stayed in the United States for as long as I could bear to be away from home, for about six weeks, and the Jews all over the country listened, wept and gave money – and when they had to, took loans from banks in order to cover their pledges.'[7] (During the two other traumatic Israeli wars of 1967 and 1973 – many American Jews again resorted to taking personal loans, mortgaging their homes and selling their jewels in order to get money to Israel in a hurry.)

In the inflation-ridden second half of the 1970s American Jews, through the United Israel Appeal, contributed a gross figure of approximately $220 million a year, of which between $190 and $200 million actually got to Israel. The $20 to $30 million difference is not because of high collection costs or other negative reasons. On the contrary, it is due to the confidence of the American banking community in the stability and word of the UJA and the UIA. When Israel needs more cash than these two organizations have in hand, they go to the banks. The banks lend them the cash immediately, purely on the basis of signed pledges by contributors in the future and UJA/UIA's impeccable repayment record in the past.

The difference between the amount raised in America and the amount sent to Israel is thus the cost of prior loans from the banks.[8]

An illustration of the lengths to which the highest Israeli officials go to treat 'big givers' to the UJA is the following excerpt from the 31 August–6 September 1980 issue of the *Jerusalem Post*'s international edition:

The 110 members of the United Jewish Appeal's Prime Minister's Mission arrived in Israel last week for four days of touring, listening and questioning.

The participants, who have each pledged at least $100,000 to the UJA this year, come from the US and Canada, and are their countries' prime [lay] fundraisers for the organization.

Welcomed by women soldiers, they went to [the village] Kfar Habad to meet Youth Aliya youngsters. [Youth Aliya is the branch of the Zionist movement charged with housing and educating orphaned, homeless, or otherwise deprived youngsters for a productive life in Israel.] They then proceeded to Beit Hanassi [the Israeli White House] in Jerusalem, where President Yitzhak Navon thanked them for their efforts.

They also attended a dinner at the Knesset [Israel's parliament] and were addressed there by Prime Minister Menachem Begin.

There are other ways of helping Israel financially. One of them is tourism. Despite acts of terror inside Israel and the generally volatile Middle Eastern political and military climate, 1,070,813 tourists visited Israel from Asia, Africa, Europe, Oceania, and North and South America in 1978. Almost 293,000 of them came from the United States – the largest number of tourists from any single country in the world.[9] Moreover the number of American Christians who visit Israel annually may now equal or exceed the number of Jews, and while most of the Jews are repeat visitors, most of the Christians are coming for the first time.[10]

Another way for American Jews to give money to Israel is to donate it directly to their favorite charity there. Thus there are separate organizations incorporated in the United States that raise tax-deductible money for specific institutions, such as Orthodox Jewish religious seminaries, each of Israel's universities, the Weizmann Institute of Science, the Israel Philharmonic, the Israel Museum, the Hadassah Hospital, and the Magen David Adom (the

Red Shield of David), the Jewish equivalent of Christendom's Red Cross and Islam's Red Crescent. That is why the 1980 edition of the *American Jewish Year Book* lists over fifty national organizations under the heading of 'Zionist and Pro-Israel', – in addition to the United Jewish Appeal, the United Israel Appeal, and the Joint Distribution Committee.

The Israeli newspaper article, cited earlier, describing the VIP welcome given to big contributors to the United Jewish Appeal ends with a paragraph which notes that a small group of demonstrators at the airport greeted the visitors with placards saying : 'We don't want donations, we want investments.' Without deprecating donations, the 'we want investments' part of the placards could very well be the slogan of the State of Israel Bonds Organization in the United States.[11]

The organization came into being in 1951 for the purpose of tapping that portion of the American community that wishes to invest in Israel rather than (or in addition to) donating to it. The motivation here is business, not charity. For its part, Israel is concerned with large amounts of long-term funds for long-range economic development projects. For their part, the buyers of the bonds are concerned with capital, risk, interest payments, and the safety of their investment. In thirty years Israel Bonds money has helped Israel to drain the malaria-ridden lakes and swamps of the Huleh Valley in northern Galilee; construct the National Water Carrier that brings water from the Sea of Galilee and the River Jordan down to the parched deserts of the south; build oil pipelines from Eilat to Haifa, Ashdod, and Ashkelon; extend facilities at each of Israel's seaports, explore for oil (with not too much success so far); develop atomic, solar, and conventional energy sources; establish new development villages and towns; create steel mills, cement plants, and other industrial enterprises; expand water desalination and water recycling projects; add new telephone exchanges and microwave and cable facilities; enlarge the nation's rail and highway systems; improve Ben-Gurion International Airport (between Jerusalem and Tel-Aviv) as well as the airports in Jerusalem, Eilat, and Haifa; and continue the exploration of such ores as ceramic clay, phosphates, bromine, magnesium, and potash.

In those same thirty years more than 2 million buyers have bought almost $5 billion worth of State of Israel Bonds. In 1979 the Israel Bonds organization in the United States produced a total of $394·5 million, which was a 24·7 million increase over the

1978 figure of $369·8 million. According to a news release issued by the Philadelphia branch of State of Israel Bonds on 7 January 1980, 'for the fifth successive year [total] cash receipts from the sale of Israel Bonds and other financial instruments showed substantial increases over previous years'. These were years in which both inflation and interest rates for borrowed money ranged into double digits. Yet so many Israel Bonds have been bought in the United States that they are one of the most widely held securities in the country. Only United States Savings Bonds and the issues of 'Ma Bell' – the American Telephone and Telegraph Company – exceed them.

This is remarkable, especially when one considers that Israel Bonds have always paid a very low rate of interest; the current rates are only 4, 5·5 and 7·5 percent. Even more remarkable is that some of America's largest companies, banks, and labor unions have bought large amounts of these securities. The corporate buyers include the Coca-Cola Company, Mack Trucks, Melville Corporation, the Borden Corporation, Allied Stores Corporation, Walter Kidde & Company, Colonial Stores, Caldor, the Michigan National Corporation, the Central Trust Company of Rochester, New York, the Manufacturers National Bank of Detroit, and the Garden State National Bank of New Jersey. Lest it be thought that these companies are headed by Jews, and that is why they buy the bonds, the names of the chief executive officers of the companies mentioned are, respectively, J. Paul Austin, Zenon C. R. Hansen, Francis C. Rooney, Jr, A. R. Marusi, Thomas Macioce, Fred R. Sullivan, Ernest Boyce, Carl Bennett, Stanford C. Stoddard, Angelo A. Costanza, Deane Richardson, and Charles A. Agemian.

The participation of American labor unions, their pension funds, and their health and welfare funds in the purchase of Israel Bonds is even more striking. In 1980 the bonds organization issued a list of about forty unions 'which hold substantial amounts [about a quarter of a billion dollars] of Israel Bonds in their portfolios'. The list (in which unions with few Jewish members are denoted by an asterisk) includes :

Amalgamated Clothing Workers of America (AFL-CIO)
Amalgamated Lithographers of America (Independent)
* Amalgamated Meat Cutters and Butcher Workmen of North
    America (AFL-CIO)
American Federation of Musicians (AFL-CIO)

Bakery and Confectionery Workers International Union of America (AFL-CIO)

* Bricklayers, Masons and Plasterers International Union of America (AFL-CIO)

Distillery, Rectifying, Wine and Allied Workers International Union of America (AFL-CIO)

Graphic Arts International Union (AFL-CIO)

Hotel and Restaurant Employees' and Bartenders' International Union (AFL-CIO)

* International Association of Bridge and Structural Iron Workers (AFL-CIO)

* International Association of Machinists and Aerospace Workers (AFL-CIO)

* International Brotherhood of Electrical Workers (AFL-CIO)

* International Brotherhood of Painters and Allied Trades of the United States and Canada (AFL-CIO)

* International Brotherhood of Teamsters, Chauffeurs, Warehousemen and Helpers of America (Independent)

International Jewelry Workers Union (AFL-CIO)

International Ladies Garment Workers Union (AFL-CIO)

International Leather Goods, Plastics and Novelty Workers Union (AFL-CIO)

* International Longshoremen's Association (AFL-CIO)

International Typographical Union (AFL-CIO)

International Union of Dolls, Toys, Playthings, Novelties and Allied Products of the United States and Canada (AFL-CIO)

* International Union of Operating Engineers (AFL-CIO)

* International Union of Wood, Wire and Metal Lathers (AFL-CIO)

* Laborers International Union of North America (AFL-CIO)

Laundry, Cleaning and Dye Houseworkers International Union (Independent)

* Longshoremen's and Warehousemen's International (Independent)

Retail Clerks International Association (AFL-CIO)

Retail, Wholesale and Department Store Union (AFL-CIO)

* Seafarers International Union of North America (AFL-CIO)

* Service Employees International Union (AFL-CIO)

* Sheet Metal Workers International Association (AFL-CIO)

Textile Workers Union of America (AFL-CIO)

* United Association of Journeymen and Apprentices of the Plumbing and Pipe Fitting Industry of the United States and Canada (AFL-CIO)
* United Automobile, Aerospace and Agricultural Implement Workers of America (Independent)
* United Brotherhood of Carpenters and Joiners of America (AFL-CIO)
  United Furniture Workers of America (AFL-CIO)
  United Hatters, Cap and Millinery Workers International Union (AFL-CIO)
* United Paperworkers International Union (AFL-CIO)
* United Steelworkers of America (AFL-CIO)

American Jews buy Israel Bonds (as they give charity to Israel) because they are Jews, because they are Zionists regardless of whether they actually belong to Zionist organizations, because they want the country to survive as prosperously and peaceably as possible, and because, like other human beings, they are susceptible to appeals to their ethnicity, their pride, their vanity, their egos, and their status within the community. But why do American Christians buy Israel Bonds?

This is something that baffles many Jews, especially those who believe that every *goy* in the world is at least a latent Jew-hater and that if you scratch the skin of a Christian long and deep enough, underneath you will find the flesh of a live anti-Semite. This is not true, of course, but bad memories and old myths die hard. While it may be suggested, particularly by foreigners not familiar with Christian–Jewish relations in the United States, that Christians buy the bonds because of various forms of pressure flowing from the linkage of economic interests between Christians and Jews, I think the suggestion, if valid at all, applies to only a small number of non-Jewish bonds buyers. The reasons that American Christians buy them is that they are, by and large, pro-Jewish and pro-Israel. Those of them who have the money to invest in the Jewish state do so to demonstrate economic solidarity with Israel, a gesture which is made easier by the fact that neither the government of Israel nor the bonds organization has ever missed a redemption date or an interest payment.

This same pro-Israelism explains why, despite desperate unsolved economic and social problems at home, three-quarters of the Americans polled in the autumn of 1980 by the respected Louis Harris

Organization 'were in favour of military aid to Israel despite the Arab threat to cut off oil supplies to the US'.[12] It is the only explanation for the $15·6 billion of both military and non-military aid that the United States has given and loaned to Israel between 1948 and 1980.[13] The military aid is especially impressive because the United States does not even have a military alliance with Israel. There is no agreement with Israel like the formal American commitments to come to the defense of Japan, South Korea, Canada, Western Europe, and most of the countries of Latin America. Nevertheless, between 1970 and 1978 the value of American military grants, sales, and military education and training to Israel was $7·6652 billion – almost 24 percent of the total of American military aid given all over the world. In the single year of 1978 America's worldwide military aid was $2·353 billion. Israel's share was $1 billion – half in grants and half in loans. For the 1981 fiscal year the American administration asked Congress to approve an addition $1·985 billion of military aid to Israel, some of it also in repayable loans.[14]

According to the *New York Times* of 7 March 1981, Israel is repaying loans to the United States at the rate of $700 million a year. These repayments, plus those to private individuals and organizations, are constant reminders of the credit noose tightening around Israel's neck. In time that credit noose, rather than the surrounding Arab states, may strangle Israel to death. Even if it does not, we do well to wonder whether so much economic dependency on a single outside source is sociologically, psychologically, and politically healthy for a people that has striven so hard to achieve and maintain its sovereignty. Perhaps this is why, when the Israeli polling organization *Modi'in Ezrachi* (Citizen Information) recently asked a representative sample of the population whether it was once and for all ready to lower drastically its standard of living in order to end this economic dependency upon America, 38·2 percent of the people answered 'yes'.[15] True, a majority answered 'no'. But if things go on as they have, the minority response may well become 'the more significant finding of the poll', in the words of the man who directed it.[16]

Three thousand five hundred years ago Moses delivered the ancient Israelites from their political bondage to the Pharaohs of Egypt. Who or what will deliver the modern Israelis from their economic bondage to the United States and their American brethren?

I0

Palestinian Terrorism and Israeli Retaliation

Israel is not the only country that has suffered from acts of terror and the Palestinians are not the only people who have committed such acts. Great Britain has the Irish Republican Army. Spain has the Basque nationalists. Italy has the Red Brigades. Turkey has the Turkish People's Liberation Army. Pakistan has its *al Zulfikar* (the Sword) group. Uruguay has the Tupamaros, who derive their name from an ancient Incan revolutionary. Ethiopia has the Eritrean Liberation Front. Japan has the United Red Army. West Germany has the Rote Armee Faktion, founded by the old Baader-Meinhof Gang. America has the Puerto Rican Fuerzas Armadas de Liberación Nacional. And Israel has the Popular Front for the Liberation of Palestine, as well as other terrorist groups – some affiliated with the PLO (the Palestine Liberation Organization) and others not.

As Jack Jacobs wrote in a letter in the August–September 1979 issue of the *Jewish Frontier*, the organ of the American Zionist group most akin to the Labor-dominated governments that have ruled Israel throughout most of its modern existence, 'The only way in which terrorism can be stopped is by ending the conflict between Jews and Palestinians'. But until that happens it is import-ant for foreigners (including American Jews) to appreciate – even if they may not always approve of – the way in which *Israelis* view Palestinian terrorism, how and why they react to it, how they react to the world's reaction to it, and especially how they react to the outside world's negative response to Israeli military retaliation. In other words, Israel believes there are good reasons for its conduct and for its perceptions of the moral, psychological, and political components of this terrible problem. What are they?[1]

First, there is the component of emotional stress caused by the ever-present danger of being killed or injured, either at home or abroad, by a Palestinian terrorist attack. It is not very pleasant for Israelis serving their country in diplomatic posts overseas generally to be forbidden by their government to live in detached private homes with gardens and grounds about them. Instead, for security reasons, they are usually obliged to live in multilevel apartment houses or flats. This is much more of a psychological deprivation than many Americans may realize. For unlike the latter, the vast majority of Israelis in Israel live in condominiums or housing cooperatives with relatively little space and privacy. The symbolic proof of this is the fact that to an Israeli almost any dwelling that has no outside walls connected to any other dwelling, and no ceilings or floors below or above any other dwelling, is, regardless of its size, usually called a villa.

It is neither comfortable nor cheap for Israeli diplomatic and commercial establishments overseas to be saddled with security precautions and paraphernalia that their counterparts from most other countries can happily do without. Within Israel itself, it certainly is not pleasant to have your purse or bag searched upon entering almost any large store or building. And if you enter such stores or buildings twenty times a day, your purse or bag will be searched twenty times a day. It is just not relaxing to have to be always on the lookout for the unattended package, the unaccounted-for suitcase. Nor is it fun to be subjected to extremely stringent body and baggage searches each time you travel by air in, to, or from Israel. And it is not the most pleasing part of parenthood to be faced with newspaper pictures and descriptions of buttons, pins, pencils, pens, marbles, and so on, which are really explosive devices in disguise. At the end of one school year the Israeli press published pictures and descriptions with such large-type headings as: 'PARENTS, STUDY THESE PAGES CAREFULLY WITH YOUR CHILDREN AND MAKE SURE THEY KNOW THEIR CONTENTS.' 'PARENTS, NOW THAT SCHOOL IS OUT FOR THE SUMMER HOLIDAYS, MAKE SURE THAT YOUR CHILDREN DO NOT PICK UP OBJECTS SUCH AS THESE FROM THE STREETS OR FROM THE FIELDS.'

My second point has to do with the words that Israelis use to refer to Palestinian terrorists. At least until recently, the outside world used to call them guerrillas or commandos. The Israelis never do. They remember that the word 'guerrilla' (little war), comes from the valiant efforts of the Spaniards to free themselves from Napoleon's domination in the early 1800s and that those efforts were directed against French soldiers and not civilians of whatever nationality. As for 'commando' – and thousands of Palestinian Jews served in the British armed forces during World War II – they consider it a very honorable word which they associate with daring military exploits by military men in uniform against military targets or other military men in uniform. To Israelis the term 'commando' conjures up heroic memories of British, or Canadian, or American units doing the kinds of military things that the laws of war permit and the lords of Hollywood sometimes make exciting films about. Since the hijacking of civilian aircraft, the shooting up of schoolhouses and schoolchildren, the massacre of passengers at airports, and the extermination of athletes at Olympic Games are not the kinds of things that real commandos do, or should do, the Israelis, in referring to Palestinian terrorists, always use the Hebrew words *mekhablim* or *teroristim* (saboteurs or terrorists).

Thirdly, contrary to conventional unwisdom abroad, Israeli soldiers have great respect for the fighting abilities of their uniformed Arab counterparts whom they meet in battle. But they have nothing but scorn for Palestinian terrorists killing civilians, be they Israelis, Arabs, or foreign visitors and tourists.

Fourthly, Israelis resent the terrorist claim that everything in Israel – including every single Jewish man, woman, and child in the country – is a legitimate military target. This is a point very often overlooked by outsiders or by casual visitors to the country. The thinking of terrorists who feel this way and act accordingly is as follows. Israeli men go into the army and serve in the reserves every year until their fifties. Israeli women also are drafted into the Israeli Army. And since every child is either male or female, he or she, upon growing up, will also enter the army. So any person not in the army now will someday be in it – or in the border police, the civil guard, or the reserves. Therefore, all Jews living in 'occupied Palestine', which to the terrorists means every square inch of Israel regardless of its borders and the year it attained them, are present or potential military targets.

Israelis resent even more the fact that many foreign governments and journalists in the democratic world appear to be letting the Palestinian terrorists get away with this military target claim. So, too, do they resent what they believe to be the double standard being applied to their situation by the outside world. The double standard goes something like this. Everyone knows that innocent people get killed in wars. If innocent Israeli men, women, and children get killed in the Ma'alot School in northern Israel or in Jerusalem's Zion Square or Makhanei Yehuda Market, that is the terribly unfortunate result of, in this case, a Palestinian Arab war of national liberation. But if, on the other hand, the Israeli Army attacks Lebanon and shells, bombs, and blows up terrorist arms caches and bases that are often deliberately placed in the middle of Palestinian refugee camps, villages, or homes (against the wishes of the fearful inhabitants of these camps, villages, and homes) – well, there go those bloodthirsty, trigger-happy, arrogant, Israelis again. In other words, when the outside world does react to Palestinian acts of terrorism and to Israeli retaliation, it does so, in the Israeli view, in the most uneven fashion. It is this double standard – not only toward Palestinian terrorism but to other things as well – that irritates Israelis most of all.

Fifthly, the tactical purpose of terrorism is to terrorize. If its strategic purpose in the case of Israel is to frighten its citizens, to disorient them, to widen existing socioeconomic cleavages, and to turn them away from their government, their patriotism, and their commitment to the renascent Jewish state, that purpose is not being achieved. In fact, the opposite has happened: terror brings disparate segments of Israeli society closer together than might otherwise be the case.

Sixthly, while Israelis take terrorism very seriously and take every possible precaution to prevent or minimize it, they are not intimidated by it. They distinguish between a threat and a thorn. Terror is a thorn – a terribly bloody and costly thorn – but it is not a real threat to their security and survival. They believe that, given the fact that the terrorists have killed many more Arabs – from peasants to prime ministers – than they have Jews, they are a far greater danger to the Arab governments that spawn, supply, and shelter them.

Seventhly, as heinous as some of the terrorists' acts have been, Israel has never imposed the death penalty on any terrorist captured alive. In fact, when the Israeli cabinet voted to do so in 1979 – a decision which has not been carried out – it aroused protests from Jews both in Israel and overseas.

Eighthly, the Israelis have never been able to understand the logic that makes Western airlines, for example, suspend flights to Israel when Israeli planes, airports, or citizens are hit by terrorists – even abroad – rather than suspending flights to the countries that hatch or harbor terrorists. Similarly, they find it incredible that, instead of boycotting the athletes and athletic events of these same terrorist-aiding countries, other nations often bar Israeli athletes from certain games for fear that their presence may attract terrorists to their countries.

Years ago the Israelis warned the world that internationally tolerated terrorism in the Middle East was a dangerously contagious virus that knows no political boundaries. If left unchecked, they said, it would spread to other causes, countries, and continents. And it has. The takeover in November 1979 of the United States embassy in Tehran and the holding there of more than fifty hostages for 444 days is only the most publicized example of how the terrorist virus has struck Americans. But there are others, some all but forgotten. Arab terrorists – whether Palestinian or not is un-known – murdered the American ambassador to the Sudan and his deputy in 1973. They did the same thing to the American ambassador to Lebanon in 1976. There may have been an Arab involvement in the murder of the American ambassador to Afghan-istan in 1979. In the late summer of 1980 there was an unsuccess-ful attempt in Beirut on the life of yet another American ambassa-dor to Lebanon. At other times in the recent past, terrorists have killed an aide to former Senator Jacob K. Javitz who was travelling in Turkey, butchered a group of Puerto Ricans who had come as pilgrims to Jerusalem, stolen and destroyed American aircraft, and letterbombed American citizens.[2] None of the known perpetrators of these acts has ever been punished by the Arab country from which they came or by the Arab country to which they fled.

So much for terrorism. What about *tagmul* (the Hebrew word for retaliation or reprisal)? Because they are secret, hard facts are hard to come by. But 600-plus is the figure that I have often heard bandied about regarding the total number of Israelis who have been killed by all kinds of terrorist activity in the three decades of modern Israel's existence. That number is not much greater than the annual number of Israelis killed in automobile accidents on the nation's streets and highways. In 1979, in addition to 600 road deaths and 100 suicides, terrorists killed twenty-three people in Israel, ten of whom were Arabs. Whatever the numbers of Jews killed by Palestin-ian terrorists, Israelis know that retaliation will not alter the demographic imbalance between Jews and Arabs in the area. They admit that retaliation does not stop terrorism. They understand that they can never be sure about its effectiveness as a deterrent. For how can they, or anyone, measure how many terrorist attacks there would be both with and without retaliation? Are there fewer attacks because the terrorists know that the Israelis always retaliate? Would there be more attacks if the terrorists knew that Israel's reaction to them would be erratic or completely non-existent?

There are even more problems associated with retaliation. Israel's political and military leaders know full well that when they retaliate by force against a terrorist attack, they bring upon themselves the condemnation of the United Nations (which they do not care about because they believe the organization is hopelessly biased against them) as well as the verbal wrath of governments they very much care about, especially the United States government. They also realize that each military response weakens the hands of those in the Arab world, including Palestinians, who want an accommodation with Israel and are ready to accept its existence in the Middle East. So, if the number of Jews that the terrorists kill is relatively tiny and the political problems raised by retaliation are relatively large, who does Israel retaliate?

Israel's desire to maintain some leverage in unstable southern Lebanon is one explanation. The duty of any government to protect its citizens from internal and external violence is another. Still another is the biblical injunction in Exodus 21 : 23–5 : 'Wherever hurt is done, you shall give life for life, eye for eye, tooth for tooth, hand for hand, foot for foot, burn for burn, bruise for bruise, wound for wound.' But the main imperative for retaliation, no matter whether outsiders believe or accept it, comes from the scars left by the Nazi Holocaust. Domestic psychopolitical pressures, the bitter historical memories of the Jewish people, and the fear that if they misstep there will be another Holocaust – this time in the Middle East – have led the leaders and citizens of Israel to believe that they have no choice except to retaliate. True, there have been different degrees of retaliation under different Israeli governments. When schoolchildren were massacred in Ma'alot the Labor government did not respond with a massive military invasion of Lebanon, whereas the Begin government did exactly that in March 1978 when Palestinian terrorists perpetrated the equally heinous massacre of a busload of Israelis caught on the Haifa–Tel-Aviv coastal road. But while the Israeli State Comptroller drew attention in his annual report to the military incompetence of the invasion – the so-called Operation Litani – and other Israelis felt that the operation was an overreaction with inappropriately high civilian casualties on the Lebanese side of the border, very few Israelis feel that the policy of reprisals should be ended while terrorists continue to kill unarmed Israeli civilians. Indeed, there is no evidence that the Israeli in the street was opposed to the Begin policy of preventative retaliation, which means selective and preemptive small-scale military strikes against known Palestinian terrorist bases in southern Lebanon, as a means of keeping the terrorists off balance.

Until the Palestinians and the Israelis – both of whom are here to stay – come to accept each other's existence and legitimacy, the vicious cycle of *teror* and *tagmul*, of terrorism and reprisal, will continue unabated, with all of its ugliness, all of its hatred, and all of its deadliness.

I I

American Jews and Israelis:
the Unequal Partners

> peo-ple – 1, the whole body of persons constituting a
> community, tribe, race, or nation because of a common
> culture, history, religion, or the like: *the people of
> Australia; the Jewish people.*
>
> *(The Random House Dictionary
> of the English Language,* 1966)

Prime Minister Menachem Begin once wrote a letter to an Ameri-
can Jew. Part of it was published in the *New York Times* of 25
July 1980. In it he said: 'I believe with all my heart that Eretz
Israel [Land of Israel] belongs to the whole Jewish people and not
only to those Jews who live in it.' In 1978 the late Moshe Dayan,
Israel's then Foreign Minister, told a meeting of the Romanian
Jewish community in Bucharest: 'I am first and foremost a Jew –
and only then an Israeli. Together we symbolize the Jewish people.'
In 1939 Eliezer Rieger, a lesser-known Israeli who was an influential
Hebrew educator in the years immediately before and after the
state's establishment, wrote:[1]

> Eretz Yisrael and the *Gola* [Hebrew for the Jews of the
> Diaspora] are mutually indispensable. Without the *Gola* to
> encompass it, Eretz Yisrael will become parochial; and without
> Eretz Yisrael as its center the *Gola* is apt to deteriorate . . .
> The Jewish settlement in Eretz Yisrael will thus be the *avant
> garde* of the Jewish People and it will have to bear the respon-
> sibility for world Judaism.

These references to the Jewish people – four among thousands in
Jewish and Zionist history – are much more than pieces of repetitive

rhetoric. They refer to a serious concept. The *Jewish people* (as the American dictionary calls them), *dos yiddishe folk* (as Yiddish speakers refer to themselves), and *am yisrael* or *ha'am ha'yehudi* (as Hebrew speakers refer to the concept) denote a transnational, multilingual, historical, and religious group which professes a oneness, a unity, a whole, a solidarity, and a partnership that predates by millennia the modern political Jewish state. The concept applies to all Jews in the world, whether they realize it or not, whether they want it to or not, and whether they like it or not. For Jewish peoplehood *is Judaism*, which is much more of an extraterritorial civilization or way of life than it is a religion in the gentile sense. And the proof of this is that no other religious group in the world so steadily and so steadfastly calls itself a people.

Do the multifarious denominations of American Protestantism, concerned as they may be with the fate of foreign Protestants, call themselves, for example, the Methodist people, the Baptist people, the Episcopalian people, or the Presbyterian people? Do American Catholics, tied as they are to foreign Catholics through such institutions as the papacy and the priesthood, call themselves the Catholic people, even though catholic is a synonym for universal? Do American Muslims, American Hindus, and American Buddhists use the word in reference to their creeds? No. Only Jews do – be they Americans, Israelis, Romanians or Australians. Also, more than any other major religion, Judaism is geocentric. Having given monotheism to the world, Judaism of course preaches belief in one universal God who watches over humankind everywhere. But for about 5,000 years that belief has been tied to a little piece of Middle Eastern territory, and almost every one of Judaism's hopes, holidays, traditions, teachings, yearnings, and rituals are linked in one way or another to what has occurred, is occurring, might occur, or will occur – the coming of the Messiah, for instance – in that little piece of territory.

In the late 1940s and the early 1950s it was not at all uncommon for American Jews to be told, Tarzan-like, by young, politically pubescent, Israeli *sabras*: 'Me Israeli, you Jew.' And when the *sabras* said it, they said it with a tone and a look deliberately designed to convey the notion that God had made them a much higher, nobler, tougher, better breed of men and women than their coreligionists in Exile. It did not matter that many of the Exiles were life-long Zionists and/or survivors of the Nazi Holocaust, which the *sabras* were lucky enough to miss. It did not matter that for many of the Americans there were good family or other reasons why they could not emigrate to Israel. Nor did it matter that many of the Diaspora Jews abroad knew a lot more about Jewish history, the Jewish religion, Jewish values, and Zionism itself than did many of these young and virile Israeli 'Canaanites', whose knowledge of Jewish events between the years 70 and 1948 is sadly deficient. They just thought, in the words of one young man whose name I have forgotten, that 'the Judaism of the *Galut* [another Hebrew term for the Diaspora] is not worthy of survival'. Fortunately, time and trauma have dissipated much of this juvenilism among Israelis of all ages. The 1973 Yom Kippur War, especially, made Israeli and non-Israeli Jews realize just how much they meant to and needed one another.

The Jews of Israel and of the Diaspora are in a sense partners in a marriage – with all the mutual love, hate, companionship, dependence, disagreement, and bickering that characterize a real marriage between two highly strung individuals facing an unfriendly world together. As in a real marriage, each partner gets something special from the other partner and each partner shares something special with the other partner. Israel gets material, moral, and political support and the Jews of America get psychological, ethnic, and religious pride. Both carry a shared memory of the Holocaust, a shared guilt that they survived, a shared fear of its repetition, and a shared determination that they must do everything in their combined power to prevent its ever happening again.

But, as in many successful real-life marriages, there is tension in the house. No fair-minded Jew in America or elsewhere can rightfully claim mathematical equality in the house of partnership with Israel. In certain matters – security decisions, for instance – Israel feels that it must be the senior partner. However, even junior partners like to be consulted beforehand rather than merely being informed afterwards. Even junior partners do not appreciate the downgrading of their work and effort for the common cause. And no partner likes to be told (as Israeli leaders often tell the leaders of American Jewry), 'be our fiscal, informational, and political shock troops in Washington. But in all other areas in which we share concerns, just leave everything to us'. Besides, partnerships have histories. It does great harm when older Israelis forget, and younger Israelis are never taught, the history of the vital political role American Jews played in Israel's birth and growth into sovereignty. And it would do much good if Israelis of all ages would heed the plea that Theodore R. Mann, a former chairman of the Conference of Presidents of Major American Jewish Organizations, addressed to them in 1979 : 'Believe in our future and act on that belief, just as we believe in your future and act on that belief.' [2]

In his book, *We Are One!*, Melvin I. Urofsky observed that 'the relations between American Jewry and Israel are composed not only of ties that bind, but of differences that sunder'. To me, the main sundering difference derives from conflicting conceptions of Jewish peoplehood and partnership, as well as from three subsidiary differences that stand out in particular. They are (1) the absence of Jewish religious pluralism in Israel, (2) the right or non-right of Jews abroad to criticize Israeli policies, and (3) the post-state duties of Diaspora Zionists, especially as regards their settling in Israel.

'Wie es sich christelt so jüdelt es sich auch.' This is a German saying that dates back at least to the Middle Ages. Freely translated, it means 'As the Christians do, so too do the Jews', and it has relevance to the differing religious mind sets of Israeli and American Jews. The latter have been nurtured under the constitutional principle of church/state separation and the tradition of religious pluralism fostered by the principle. Under it, not only Orthodox Jews, but Conservative, Reform, Reconstructionist, and completely secular Jews have been able to live Jewishly in the manner of their choice. But Israeli Jews, the vast majority of whom are secular and non-observant, live under a nonconstitutional, but very definitely enforced, semifusion of synagogue and state. Under this semifusion, Orthodox Judaism is the only legally recognized branch of Judaism. This places distressing burdens on secular Jews and poses a dilemma for non-Orthodox religious Jews who, like their Orthodox brethren, also believe and recite the prayer : 'For out of Zion shall go forth the Torah [the Five Books of Moses], and the word of the Lord from Jerusalem.' The founder of Reconstructionist Judaism, Rabbi Mordecai M. Kaplan, who grew up in America but now lives in Israel, put the dilemma this way : [3]

On the one hand, they will not concede to the [Orthodox] Rabbinate, or any other religious body [the Ministry for Religious Affairs, for example], political authority in the Government of Israel. And on the other hand, they can't maintain the continuity of Judaism as a religious civilization without religion as an integral part of Jewish life. They have to find a way of imbuing the Jewish community of Israel, which is the hub of the Jewish people throughout the world, with the spirit of religion without being theocratic.

Kaplan believes that the 'Orthodox would mold Israel into a theocracy', and if not stopped they will continue to 'impose their will on the rest of the community'.

But Israel is not a theocracy. It has a complete civil court system, capped by a High Court of Justice that can exert its will over the Chief Rabbinate, the religious courts, and the Ministry for Religious Affairs. Yet Mordecai Kaplan is essentially correct. Then how did it happen that the Orthodox have been able to impose their will on the rest of the community? It happened because the Israeli electorate has to date never given any political party enough seats in parliament to rule alone. Every Prime Minister from Ben-Gurion to Begin depended upon the religious bloc to form a functioning coalition government.[4] Coalition government necessarily means compromise politics. The compromises on religion have been more in the direction of the Orthodox elements than their relatively small numbers in the cabinet, the Knesset, and the overall population would warrant.

As a result, the recognition and registration of all matters of 'personal status' – birth, death, marriage, divorce, remarriage, intermarriage, religion, conversion, and the like – are in the hands of the clerics of each of the religions in Israel. For Jews this means that their personal status, especially what is permissible and what is not permissible under Jewish religious law, is determined by the Orthodox-dominated Interior Ministry, the Ministry for Religious Affairs, the Chief Rabbinate, and the rabbinical courts. Thus:

- The Orthodox establishment determines who is and who is not a Jew and which Jewish immigrants are entitled to early Israeli citizenship under the Law of Return.
- Reform, Conservative, and Reconstructionist rabbis living in Israel cannot be appointed to the religious courts.
- They cannot serve in the army's chaplaincy corps.
- They cannot perform marriages, grant divorces, conduct funerals, or induct converts into Judaism, and if they do so in Israel their acts are not recognized by either the religious or civil authorities.
- Any such acts performed by them abroad may or *may not* be recognized in Israel – a real problem when the individuals in-

volved, or their descendants, decide to settle in the country.

• Since there is no civil marriage or divorce, those Jews who cannot receive one can, if they have the money, travel abroad for the proper ceremony, hoping upon their return that it will be recognized and registered at home. For if it is not, they may be considered adulterers or bigamists and their children illegitimate.

• Non-Orthodox congregations in Israel – and there may be as many as fifty of them – have no legal standing as religious institutions and are also barred from receiving financial and other support which the state supplies to other religious institutions.

• On the Sabbath and on the major Jewish holy days public places of entertainment are closed, the public buses do not run – but private taxis do – and streets containing synagogues and neighborhoods populated by Orthodox Jews are closed to all cars by the police.

• Full-time male students at *yeshivot* (Orthodox religious academies or seminaries) may be permanently exempted from military service, as may any Orthodox Jewish female if she or her family requests it.

Because military service – both in the standing army and in the reserves – is a way of life in Israel, exemption on religious grounds is perhaps the single most rankling issue within the synagogue/state controversy among the Jews who live in the country. There are Israeli families in which one or more members have been killed in each of the major wars – 1948, 1956, 1967 and 1973 – not to mention actions not labelled as wars. One of my women students at Temple University lost three brothers to military action between 1973 and 1980.

Even those who have not lost close relatives are outraged. A decade ago Leonard Perlov, an American immigrant with two army-age children, wrote this letter which was published in the *Jerusalem Post*:

There is a basic injustice in a system which allows certain elements of our population to evade their responsibilities to their country's defense by virtue of their religious practices. In this case, however, they claim special privileges by raising the cry of 'status quo' instead of 'halacha' [Jewish religious law]. 'Status quo' justifies exempting yeshiva students from army service, and keeps their girls safely at home, while other people's children defend our borders.

Some of these very same persons supported the resolution at the NRP [National Religious Party] convention calling for their party's withdrawal from the government if certain territories are returned to Arab rule as a result of the bargaining which will take place when peace negotiations start. To me it seems a case of unmitigated gall that those who choose to keep their children from serving in Israel's defense should attempt to influence the government toward a policy which could easily delay the peace for years to come, thereby necessitating further sacrifices by those who serve in its defense.

In 1972, when *yeshiva* students harassed Ashkenazic Chief Rabbi Shlomo Goren for a decision he had handed down, the late Prime Minister Golda Meir issued a cabinet statement of unheard-of bluntness:

It seems to me that young men (like the ones who tried to assault the Chief Rabbi last week) were not exempted from Army service in order to be free to fight their own battles. Why should these young men be free so that they can intimidate Rabbi Goren? The yeshivot exist for the sake of studying Tora, and not to make it possible for young men to roam the streets assaulting people. These young men would be wise to realize that they cannot act as they fancy as though there were no government in Israel. I hope this behaviour will stop. But if the hooliganism continues, we shall have to discuss the question [of army exemptions] particularly in those yeshivot whose students will be found to have participated in this behaviour.

The issue of exempting those religious girls who want exemptions both from the army and from alternative forms of civilian national service is even more emotional – on both sides. Partly it is due to the honest desire of some Orthodox parents to keep their daughters home in a semicloistered atmosphere until they are married. Partly it is due to the known fact that while many truly religious girls gladly serve in the army, others who are not observant at all don the cloak of religiosity to evade the draft. And partly it is due to the practice of some religious parents, who refuse to let their girls go to the army but who send these same daughters to universities away from home, let them vacation abroad without chaperons, or work in civilian offices and attend parties at night with unattached men.

The emotional dimensions of the problem from the woman's viewpoint are nicely summarized by two women – one religious and the other not – who served in the army. The first is Lieutenant Ora Mor, who comes from a religious kibbutz where all the female members have served in the army. In the February 1971 issue of *Israel Magazine* she said : 'It is not very ethical to make a cats-paw of religion. There is nothing in the Bible to keep people from joining the army. On the contrary, the Scriptures say that, in a war for survival, *everyone* must go out to fight – "the groom from his chamber and the bride from under her canopy".'

The second woman is Ziviah Ben-Shalom, a journalist and a confirmed secularist. In March 1972 she published a bitter article in the official organ of the Labor Zionist Alliance of the United States presumably because she wanted her views to be read in English by American Jews.

In the article she wrote :

The exemption of religious girls from the draft insults the army. What happens within its tents that may corrupt a decent Jewish daughter? Presumably, it is a place of wild orgies, co-ed sleeping quarters and bathrooms . . . [The] drafted girl is undressed and made to do a 'kozatzka' in the officers' dining room. Or she is forced to engage in mass-orgies. That's what goes on in the Israeli Army. Don't you know that? Where have you been? I don't want to deal with the insult to the army – let the Minister of Defense worry about that! But I need not be silent about the insult to myself. If I wanted to create a scandal and to become famous, I would bring suit against those who make certain announcements by which they are saying that I am not worthy of establishing a Jewish home and family. They imply that I am irresponsible because during twenty-four months, I wore khaki clothes . . . Not only the women are being insulted – not merely those who have served in the army, are serving, and are being mobilized for service – but also their parents who are ready to surrender their daughters; and also the men who are later prepared to marry them and establish Jewish homes and families.

Finally, she asks the anti-military-service-for-women Orthodox zealots :

Is this your opinion of our daughters? Do you value their character and morality so lightly? Place so little confidence in their education? Are you so quick to disgrace their parents who raised them to pursue 'mitzvot' [good deeds] and decent behavior? You are not ready to give her your confidence; to be sure that she will observe the Sabbath in a worldly society. . . . But if she is emotionally ready to have pre-marital relationships with a man, she will do so in civilian life.

Even when the government overlooks the law requiring religiously exempted girls to do their national service, usually near their homes, in hospitals, schools and welfare institutions – and the government has always overlooked it – and tries instead to get them to volunteer for nonmilitary service, it faces the anguished cries of the ultra-Orthodox. Whenever this happens, the government backs down.

There are of course nonmilitary examples of ultra-Orthodox domination over the lives of Jews in Israel and in the Diaspora. Reform Rabbi Roland B. Gittelsohn has written about two of them. In the May 1980 issue of the *Jewish Frontier*, he begins an article with two scenarios.[5]

Scenario 1 : There was grim foreboding in her brother's voice. The very fact that he was calling her in Boston from Israel indicated an emergency. Two sentences later, mystery was replaced by heartache. He had phoned to tell her their father had just died.

Her immediate concern was to reach Israel in time for the funeral. Would her brother arrange a delay to make that possible? Two hours later he called again. The answer of the rabbinic authorities he had consulted was that such a postponement could indeed be granted for a son, not for a daughter.

Scenario 2 : The daughter of a Reform rabbi living in Jerusalem was to be married. Because he isn't Orthodox, her father could not officiate. A liberal Orthodox rabbi agreed to stand by while the bride's father in effect conducted the ceremony, then to sign the official documents, that they might be acceptable to the rabbinate and State. The wedding was scheduled for the courtyard of the Hebrew Union College–Jewish Institute of Religion. Upon learning of the location, the Chief Rabbi of Jerusalem, whose approval was essential, balked; he would not authorize even an Orthodox rabbi to officiate on the premises of a Reform institution. Only after being threatened with a law suit filed before the High Court did the Chief Rabbi partially relent. He signed the necessary form, but listed the ceremony to take place 'in a courtyard near the King David Hotel'.

He then reports that neither scenario is fictional :

The woman who was denied attendance at her father's funeral is a veteran Hebrew teacher at Temple Israel of Boston. The Reform rabbi who needed so much ingenuity to plan his daughter's wedding is Richard Hirsch, executive director of the World Union for Progressive Judaism. Both incidents occurred in recent months. They have, moreover, been duplicated many times.

Jews both in Israel and in the Diaspora have been reluctant to go to the barricades over the Orthodox stranglehold on religion. But that reluctance evaporated a few years ago. Spurred on by the American Reform and Conservative movements and their Israeli allies, the World Zionist Organization passed the following resolution at its 29th Congress, which met in Jerusalem between 20 February and 1 March 1978.[6]

Equal Status and Identical Treatment for Every Religious Movement Affiliated with the WZO
The Congress confirms that all departments, authorities and programs of the WZO in Israel will be managed in accordance with the principle of equal status and identical treatment for every religious movement which is affiliated with the WZO, and for every Jew, regardless of his origin or his religious or ideological identification. Programs of a religious and educational character shall represent the pluralism which characterizes Jewish life throughout the world.

The Congress calls upon the State of Israel, as the homeland of the Jewish people, to put into practice the principle of assuring full rights, including equal recognition, for all rabbis, and equal assistance to all the trends in Judaism.

This began a point-counterpoint sequence which still continues. For example, just before Rosh Hashanah and Yom Kippur of 1979 the Israeli Conservative movement ran advertisements in the papers.

Under the heading 'The Jewish Heritage Does Not Belong Exclusively to Extreme Orthodox Groups But to Every Jew', they invited Israelis to worship with them in their congregations in Israel. Angered by this, Jerusalem's Chief Rabbis Bezalel Zolti and Shalom Mashash ran counteradvertisements forbidding Jews to do so. In turn, one of Israel's most prominent wags asked in print: if we can't worship in a Conservative synagogue, 'Is it okay if we just *sit* there?' On 27 February 1980 the Jewish Community Relations Council of Greater Philadelphia, one of the oldest in the nation, officially noted its 'satisfaction' with the religious pluralism resolution passed by the 29th World Zionist Congress. But it also noted that 'non-Orthodox Judaism [still] continues to suffer second-class status in Israel'. In May 1980 the Labor Zionist Alliance in America published an 'LZA Statement on Religious Pluralism' in its magazine, *Jewish Frontier*.

To: Shimon Peres, Chairman
    Israel Labor Party
The National Executive Committee of the Labor Zionist Alliance expresses its keen disappointment with the recent action of the Knesset that would transfer some of the functions of the Ministry of Religion to the Chief Rabbinate, notably in the matter of appointments of rabbis and in the recognition of marriages. The National Executive Committee is particularly disappointed that the Israel Labor Party saw fit to support this retrogressive legislation. Taken in the context of the present situation within Israeli society, this action was, in our view, aimed at preserving an anachronism which must be removed if the desires of the majority of the Jews in Israel and of the great majority of Jews in the United States are to be respected.

Religious pluralism is an idea whose time has come in Israel, too, and it is, in our view, one of the major goals to be achieved in the near future by any democratically elected regime that is not based on political alliances of doubtful merits.

The continued linkage of religion and politics, as the aforementioned legislation implies, foreshadows continued dissatisfaction with the regulation of personal status of Jews within the State of Israel, and is a deterrent to aliyah [immigration] and normal absorption of Jews from democratic countries where such clerical dictation is unknown.

We ask you to take into more serious consideration the views of Reform and Conservative Jews, as well as others, including liberal Orthodox Jews, who feel that until full freedom of choice in this area is obtained, they shall at least have recourse to the courts of Israel rather than the Rabbinate, which excludes other normative forms of Jewish expression.

As the Labor Party, hopefully, may soon return to head the Government of Israel, it is both practical and morally desirable that the jurisdiction of a non-governmental agency such as the Chief Rabbinate be curtailed, so that modifications in keeping with the wishes of the majority may more easily be implemented in the days ahead.

March 1980

The statement is important for two reasons. The LZA is the American ideological sister of the Labor Party in Israel. And the Labor Party may indeed rule Israel again when Menachem Begin or his successor falls from power.

The same issue of the same Labor Zionist magazine contains these statements by Rabbi Gittelsohn : 'If we mean what we say, if we believe our own rhetoric [about the worldwide partnership of the Jewish people], it follows ineluctably that American Zionists must speak out about the absence of religious liberty for all Jews in Israel.' He continues :

Whether Israel becomes a beacon of democracy in the Middle East or a narrow, religiously fanatic and fundamentalist pale like the Moslem societies surrounding it – this must vitally affect not only our morale but also our security. If Israel should ultimately deny the Jewishness of those who have been converted to Judaism by non-Orthodox rabbis, everything we have said about peoplehood and unity becomes a grotesque charade.

Four months later, in the fall of 1980, again on the eve of Judaism's most Holy Days, the Chief Rabbis of Jerusalem and their allies returned to the religious barricades. But this time they went far beyond their earlier warning against worshipping together with Conservative Jews. This time the Association of Rabbis in Israel placed the following advertisement in the press.

We wish to state that, in accordance with our holy torah, it is forbidden to participate in prayers held by the *Mesorati* ('Conservative') movement. One cannot fulfill one's holy obligations [in this manner], either on the High Holy Days or during the year.

We, therefore, issue this holy appeal to the public not to be tempted by the propaganda of the movement, not to participate in any of their activities, and not to associate with them.[7]

Orthodox Jews consider Reform Jews so far beyond the pale of legitimate Judaism that the advertisement did not even mention them. About 80 percent of overseas purchases of Israel Bonds and philanthropic contributions to Israeli causes comes from Reform, Conservative, and other non-Orthodox Jews. But if you are a true believer, financial facts of such magnitude do not matter.

This last episode by the Orthodox establishment prompted Eliezer Whartman, a Philadelphian who came to fight in Israel's Independence War of 1948 and stayed there ever since, to compare the religious situation in Israel with that of the early Puritans in America. 'It is ironic', he wrote, 'that Israel has taken the same path America took when the early settlers, fleeing religious persecution, promptly re-established religious bigotry within their new homeland.' Imploring American Jewry to speak out against Israeli religious bigotry, he related a conversation he had with Ashkenazic Chief Rabbi Shlomo Goren shortly after Goren was elected to his post.

'Do you regard yourself as the spiritual leader of all Israeli Jews?' I asked.

'Certainly', he replied.

'Then why don't you recognize Conservative and Reform rabbis and accord them the same rights as Orthodox rabbis?' I asked. Goren thought for a moment and replied:

'If they would be willing to accept the status of a separate sect . . . such as the Samaritans or the Karaites, I would agree to recognize them.'

'But we're speaking of the majority of the Jews in the world', I pointed out. 'You can't simply write them out of the Jewish fold.'

'As far as I am concerned', Goren rejoined, 'there is only one authentic version of Judaism. The other have no validity.'

If 'both definition and reality dictate that American Jews, especially . . . Zionists, have too great a stake in Israel to remain silent',[8] it follows that they must speak out. To speak out publicly is to criticize publicly. Until recently this was something most Jews who did not live in Israel were loath to do. I was one of them.

In December 1972 I traveled to Israel to conduct interviews and gather material for a book I later published on the noncombat impact of the Israeli Army upon Israeli society. I returned home to America with a terrible foreboding. It was that a combination of concern for their post-retirement careers, general complacency, selective perception, self-satisfaction, and downright contempt for the fighting ability of some of the Arab armies had left many of the senior officers of Israel's standing army psychologically unprepared for any new war. The foreboding was not diminished by my impression of the arrogant overconfidence of Major-General Eliahu Ze'ira, then chief of military intelligence, with whom I had talked at length on Christmas Eve. He said that only military intelligence was responsible for the formal and official intelligence estimates that were presented to the cabinet. He freely admitted that 'if we are right, we are very right. But if we are wrong, we are very wrong.'

As we know, he was very wrong. He was wrong in his assessment of enemy intentions. He was wrong in his assessment of enemy capabilities. He was wrong in his evaluation of enemy strategy and tactics. He was wrong in his steadfast refusal even to consider contrary evaluations submitted by a junior intelligence officer. And he was wrong in promising the Prime Minister and the government that he would always be able to give them warning of any impending attack in plenty of time to enable them to call up the full reserve army. No wonder that the so-called Agranat Commission, the official body (named after the then president of the Israeli Supreme Court) that Israel established soon after the 1973 war to look into preparedness shortcomings before the war concluded : 'It is our opinion that in view of his grave failures Major-General Ze'ira can no longer continue in his role as chief of Military Intelligence.' [9]

I derive no satisfaction from the congruence between my prewar foreboding and the postwar findings of the Agranat Commission. I am just angry with myself for not having had the courage then to communicate privately what other foreign Zionists are now communicating publicly even in the 'forbidden areas' of Israel's physical security and survival.

On the eve of Passover 1978 a group of thirty-seven prominent American Jews, describing themselves as 'lifelong friends of Israel', publicly supported Shalom Achshav (Peace Now), an Israeli group opposed to the peace and territorial policies of Premier Begin. In an open letter, reported in the *New York Times* of 21 April 1978, they wrote: 'We share your view that a secure peace is more important than a Greater Israel.'

Since then other 'lifelong friends of Israel' have found it necessary and appropriate to criticize it openly, especially as regards continuing Jewish settlement of the disputed West Bank of Jordan at a time when much of the northern and southern parts of Israel proper still remain relatively empty of Jews. Most Americans would, I think, agree with the American philosopher Eric Hoffer, a Christian lover of Israel, who in his 1979 book, *Before the Sabbath*, wrote: 'It does not make sense for a non-Israeli, however knowledgeable, sensitive, and benevolent, to tell Israel what to do in order to survive.' But I do not agree with Hoffer. I believe that, first, it would not have been necessary for American Jews to feel compelled to 'go public' if Israel had welcomed private constructive criticism from knowledgeable, sensitive, and benevolent Jews in the past, as it now says it is willing to do in the present and the future. Secondly, I reject entirely the Israeli contention that only those who live in the country can see and assess its problems and their solution most clearly and correctly. Just as the Frenchman, Alexis de Tocqueville, made observations about America in the nineteenth century that are still valid today, a knowing foreign Jew may know more about Israel than Israelis themselves. In other words, there is much to be said for the value of perspective, angle, focus, light, detachment – and distance.

The same 29th World Zionist Congress that resolved to push for religious pluralism in Israel resolved, as have all World Zionist Congresses, to work for the Ingathering of the Jewish people into the ancient homeland. The call for the Ingathering is a sacred tenet of Zionism. To the extent that it is successful – and it has not been successful, particularly in the affluent and democratic countries of the West – the Ingathering makes Zionism a self-liquidating movement and negates the Diaspora. This raises two questions. Who is the better, more Jewish, Jew – the one who chooses to live in Israel or the one who chooses not to? And what is, or should be, the proper *modus vivendi* between those in the homeland and those in the Diaspora?

Israelis say they want the American Jews to settle in Israel. On the conceptual and abstract level, there is no doubt that they mean it. But on the practical level, problems arise, mainly of jealousy. The jealousy derives from the way socioeconomic mobility works in Israel. For the native-born *sabra* or the long-time immigrant, job and status advancement occurs vertically, not horizontally. One is usually forced to choose one's vocational or career ladder early and one usually stays on that ladder – climbing it quickly, slowly, or not at all – for the rest of one's productive life. Exceptions are made, but only for respected retired military officers – and for Western immigrants, who are often granted housing, job, import duty, and other privileges not available to other Israelis. It is only natural, therefore, for an oldtimer who has had to break his back to buy an apartment with a short-term high-interest mortgage to resent someone else who gets a better flat on better terms. It is even more natural for someone who has waited long and worked hard for a promotion or a new job in academia, in government, or in business to be upset if one day he learns that it has been given to a new immigrant. If in his heart he knows that the new immigrant is much more qualified that he is, it will not only shatter his dreams, but it may turn temporary disappointment into permanent bitterness. To avoid this, Israelis (like other people in the same situation) will sometimes turn to intrigue. One of Israel's universities once invited a distinguished American Jewish professor to spend his sabbatical year there completely at its expense. So long as he said nothing of his interest in an academic appointment in Israel, everyone was happy and everything was fine. But as soon as he let it be known that he would accept an appointment if one were offered to him, his Israeli maid prayed that he would get it and his Israeli colleagues plotted that he would not. He did not.

In spite of this kind of occurrence, the majority of Israelis are willing to receive more immigrants from America regardless of the additional sacrifices they may have to make. But it is precisely this willingness that generates so much dismay at the reluctance of large numbers of American Jews, especially Zionist leaders, to move to Israel. In 1978, for instance, fewer than 3,000 American Jews entered the country as immigrants or potential immigrants. It seems that American Jews will send money to Israel. They will visit Israel. They will work for Israel. They will speak up for Israel. They will worry about Israel. They have even fought and died for Israel. But they will not live their lives in Israel. This puzzles and angers some

Israelis, and the puzzlement and anger erupt in ways that are both fair and unfair.

One of the fairer critics is Hillel Halkin, a former New Yorker who now lives in the Israeli town of Zichron Ya'akov. In his book, *Letters to an American Jewish Friend*,[10] which he subtitles 'a Zionist's polemic', Halkin writes:

> There is an unavoidable tension in the relationship between an Israeli Jew and a Diaspora Jew, a relationship which is ideally an adversary one since the Israeli is living in a community of faith which holds that it alone is the natural place for a Jew to live, and this tension can only be resolved by dealing with it directly. A Diaspora Jew and an Israeli can talk to each other as ordinary human beings about anything they wish, but if they are to talk to each other meaningfully as Jews, there is only one relevant question with which such a conversation can begin: Why don't you really come home?
>
> I am not saying that you cannot live an authentic Jewish life in the Diaspora; I am saying that if the criterion is the future of the Jewish people, you are living it in the wrong place. Because today, in the last quarter of the twentieth century, the survival of the Jews and the survival of Israel are the same; and whether Israel can survive depends, among other things, on the numbers and talents of Diaspora Jews who come to it.
>
> If we in Israel succeed, the long march that began nearly a century ago in Europe will be over. *We* will be home again. We will become like the Gentiles, an ordinary people with an ordinary culture of its own, which is like, in the words of the psalm, 'a tree planted by streams of water that yields its fruit in season and its leaf does not wither'. On that day there will be no need to ask anymore who is a Jew and who is an Israeli, or what is the difference between them, because the two words will have come to mean a single thing.

Others have been less fair than Hillel Halkin. In August 1979 Andrew Young, who is black, resigned from his post as the American ambassador to the United Nations because the fact that he had had an unauthorized meeting with a representative of the Palestine Liberation Organization (PLO) found its way into public print. Despite President Carter's statement that the Jews had absolutely nothing to do with Young's resignation, some American blacks

thought otherwise. Yet, right in the middle of some tense days between the leaders of these two American ethnic groups Israel's
English language newspaper (which is read by American Jews and
Christians without a command of Hebrew) published a cartoon
showing two men talking to one another as follows.[11]

First man :   And now *American* Jewry holds its breath . . .
                and braces itself for an anti-Semitic outburst.
                And the Jews of America *still* won't come
                home to Israel. And it's *our* fault that they
                won't come here. Our fault ? ! ! How is it *our*
                fault[?]
Second man : We're too 'rude and pushy' for them.

Unfairer still are some remarks attributed to a faculty member of
the Hebrew University of Jerusalem, which appeared in the *New
York Times* of 25 July 1980. One of the items covered in the *Times*
article was a Jerusalem conference between Israelis and Americans
in which the Israeli professor 'recalled fighting in the 1973 war,
lying in an Egyptian mango grove near the Suez Canal, with
shelling and sniper fire coming in'. Then he said :

All of a sudden what should appear but a big red UJA bus . . .
They got out of the bus with their cameras and their back-
slapping – nice American young people – and they took
pictures of our positions and we shared our rations with them,
and exchanged jokes, and after about 40 minutes they got on
the bus and rode out. And you can imagine how we felt after
they rode out. And that's been happening to us over and over.
You ride out.

The professor's remarks, while understandable in the military
circumstance in which he and his comrades found themselves, were
terribly unfair to the United Jewish Appeal delegation. For no one
goes anywhere in the occupied territories or in Israel itself that the
army declares off limits. Absolutely no one can just pick up and
drive a busload of people down to the Suez Canal in the middle of
a war without the prior knowledge, approval, and escort of the
Israeli Army. If a busload of American Jews appeared 'all of a
sudden' at an Egyptian mango grove, it appeared because the army
at the behest of the government wanted them there. If an Israeli

under the stress of battle wants to complain about what was probably a gauche thing to allow, he should do so. But he should send
his complaint to the right address. Also, because the critic is a
scholar, he ought to have shown more awareness of both world and
Jewish history in the matter of immigration and emigration.

Migration has almost never been a 'pull' phenomenon. Instead, it
has usually been a 'push' phenomenon. I mean by this that people
who are satisfied with their lot in life do not usually exchange their
native land for some other land. The ones who do are driven to it by
economic necessity or by political, racial, or religious persecution.
Furthermore, except for the most idealistic of individuals, or those
whose very life and limb are in immediate jeopardy, people do not
easily or often move from a country where they enjoy a higher
standard of living to one where they will face a lower standard of
living. All other things aside, most Jews in the West have a higher
living standard than most Jews in Israel and the contrast is not lost
upon the Jews in the West.

This point was noted as early as 1901, only a few years after the
formation of the World Zionist Organization, by the American
Christian minister, Maltbie Davenport Babcock. Babcock was the
pastor of New York City's Brick Presbyterian Church, and in a letter
which he wrote from Palestine he said : 'What the future has in
store for them [the Zionists] who can say? It does not seem as
though anything but bitterest anti-Semite persecution could drive
Jews from Germany, England, and America to this land, dear as it
must be to them . . . if the doors should be again opened.' [12] Babcock was correct : the Jews of these countries did not and do not
come.

In the annals of Zionism there are five heralded waves of Jewish
immigration to Palestine from 1882 to 1939. In the first wave
(1882–1903) 25,000 came, principally from Eastern Europe. In the
second wave (1904–14) 40,000 came. The third wave began after
World War I in 1919 and lasted until 1923. More than 35,000
came in that wave. The fourth wave (1924–8) numbered 67,000
immigrants, more than half of them from Poland. The only wave
that brought in a significantly larger number was the fifth one
(1929–39) when, because of the worldwide economic depression and
the rise of Adolf Hitler, more than 250,000 came, a quarter of them
from Nazi Germany. Even so, in fifty-seven years, during which
time, except for the World War I years, it was relatively easy for
Jews to get into Palestine if they wanted to, only about 417,000

did so. And most of the ones who came before 1929 did not stay.[13]

This immigration pattern was true even in antiquity. From the beginning of the Babylonian Captivity in 586 BCE to the Roman destruction of the Second Temple in 70 CE most Jews, even when given an opportunity to return to Palestine, did not. Instead they remained in other parts of the ancient world. When King Cyrus of Persia allowed Ezra and Nehemiah to lead the Jews back to Palestine and rebuild the Temple which the Romans later destroyed, the group that stayed behind was much larger than the group that went along. The numerical importance of the Diaspora in antiquity was matched by its intellectual vigor. Thus when it came time for the sages to pick *the* Talmud for use in evolving post-Torah Jewish law and theology, the one they picked was not the one that was written in Palestine, but the one that was written in Babylonia.

That Israelis should want massive immigration is entirely understandable, especially in the light of the massive population disparity between them and their surrounding enemies. But their denigration of the Diaspora flies in the face of past history and present realities. It would be helpful all around if present-day citizens of Israel – including former Americans who have 'made good' there – would recall these words of Eliezer Rieger, an Israeli from an earlier period whom I mentioned earlier.[14]

Anyone who has eyes in his head cannot help seeing that Eretz Yisrael cannot possibly absorb the myriad of Jews in *Galut* [Diaspora] . . . More powerful nations than we are – Germans, Poles, Italians, Irish, Greeks, etc. – cannot absorb their nationals in their own countries . . . Why then should we delude ourselves with impossible expectations and discourage the Hebrew *Gola* [Diaspora] that wants to live? . . . [During] the era of the Second Temple . . . [the] Jews outside Eretz Yisrael exercised a great influence upon those within it. And equally great was the prestige of Eretz Yisrael among the Jews outside.

It would be even more helpful if every Israeli who thumbs his nose at the Jews of the Diaspora in general and at those of America in particular would realize, once and for all, that if Jewish peoplehood means anything it means mutual respect by and for all members of the peoplehood no matter where in the world they have chosen to reside.

12

The Geopolitics of Population

> Since the 1967 Six-Day War . . . Israel [has been] administering the Sinai, the Golan Heights, Judaea and Samaria (also referred to as 'the West Bank'), and the Gaza District. These areas . . . have a population of more than one million Arabs.
>
> (Israel's Coordinator of Government Operations in the Administered Territories, October 1979)

> Israel's population at the eve of the New Year stood at 3,885,000 of whom 631,000 are non-Jews.
>
> (Israel's Central Bureau of Statistics, September 1980) [1]

When Israel captured 26,000 square miles of Arab territory in 1967 many people wondered why its forces did not go on to capture the capitals of the countries involved: Amman in Jordan, Cairo in Egypt, and Damascus in Syria. Why, they asked, did Israel not try to gain the political fruits of its military victories? The question has psychological and historical validity, for the capture of their capitals has in the past usually shocked vanquished countries into suing for peace. But the question cannot apply to Israel. The population of Cairo is at least 6 million, that of Damascus is over 1 million, and Amman has at least 672,000 people in it. A single country whose entire population is less than 4 million simply does not have the manpower to occupy three cities with almost 8 million inhabitants.

There is another way to look at Israel's demography. Its entire purpose is to be a Jewish state – the world's only Jewish state. It cannot be, or remain, a Jewish state without a Jewish majority. Yet within Israel proper there is a large and growing Arab minority. That is why, even if the external threat to its existence had never materialized, even if tomorrow the threat were to disappear forever, the politics of population – immigration, emigration, natural increase, and the internal demographic balance – is as vital to Israel's existence as it is limiting to Israel's options.

In 1947 there were only 630,000 Jews in all of British Palestine west of the River Jordan. On 15 May 1948, the day the Jews proclaimed their independence in partitioned Palestine, there were only 650,000 Jews in Israel. Six months later there were 717,000. In 1948 the number of Israeli Arabs, mostly Muslims, was 156,000. Between 1949 and 1978 1½ million Jews came to the new Jewish state. But during that same period the Israeli Arab population grew faster than the Israeli Jewish population : 16 percent for the one and 13·6 percent for the other. Moreover, while the Jewish rise in population in the last thirty-odd years is due in equal measure to both immigration and natural increase, the Arab population rise is almost entirely due to natural increase alone. During her lifetime the average Israeli Jewish woman at present bears 2·8 children. Her Israeli Arab Christian counterpart bears 3·0 children. But her Israeli Arab Muslim counterpart bears 6·3 children. That explains why in the 1979–80 Jewish calendar year 3,254,000 Jewish Israelis bore only 45,000 children, while 631,000 Arab Israelis gave birth to 21,000 children. The non-Jewish minority is thus reproducing itself more than twice as fast as the Jewish majority.

At this rate, according to a Hebrew University study which assumed that annexed East, or Arab, Jerusalem would remain Israeli and that Jewish immigration would continue at an average of 10,000 people a year, the Arabs living in pre-1967 Israel would make up more than a fifth of the 5,268,000 Israelis projected for 1995. If this projection holds true, the Arabs of Israel will have done almost as well in fifty years as the Francophones in Canada have done in more than two hundred. When the Protestant British conquered New France in the eighteenth century, only about 60,000 French-speaking Catholics stayed on as British subjects. Like Israel, Canada became a country of great immigration, almost none of it from France. Yet, by means of what they call *la revanche du berceau* (the revenge of the cradle), the French Canadians have by now become more than a quarter of that country's total population. I do not contend that there has been a deliberately inspired revolt of the cradle by Israel's Arabs. What is apparent is that the cradle is taken out of storage and used more often in the Arab homes of Israel than in the Jewish homes, with interesting statistical ramifications.

What I have so far described about population patterns in Israel is by no means the whole statistical picture. With occasional highs and lows in the curves, the annual number of Jewish immigrants – including immigrants from the Soviet Union – is falling, and the annual number of Jewish emigrants is rising. In 1979–80, for instance, 28,000 immigrants entered Israel and 12,000 emigrants left it. As pointed out in an earlier chapter, this is not a new phenomenon in Zionist history : it has happened before. In 1926 more than half of the Jews who came to Palestine that year did not stay. In 1927 Jewish emigration from Palestine exceeded Jewish immigration to Palestine for the first time. And these were years before the global Great Depression and the coming to power of Hitler in Germany. But the 1926–27 migration patterns occurred before a whole generation of Hebrew-speaking Israelis was born and raised in a free, democratic, and independent state of its own.

Today the psychological set is quite different, and it shows in the Hebrew terminology that Israelis use in describing their demography. When immigration and emigration do not involve Jewish settlement in Israel, the word used is *hagirah*, which can also mean migration without any reference to direction. But when we are dealing with Jews moving to or away from Israel, the words used are respectively *aliyah* and *yeridah*. They literally mean ascent and descent. How they came to be used in connection with immigration and emigration is not entirely clear. Perhaps the usage comes from the Biblical 'going down to Egypt' and 'going up to Zion'. In its modern-day Zionist context, however, Jewish immigration to Israel often connotes ascending to the highest heights of honor and Jewish emigration from Israel, descending to the deepest depths of degradation.

Israelis often make jokes about Israeli emigrants, like the one reported in the *New York Times* of 13 June 1980.

An affluent Israeli has decided to emigrate from Israel, the joke goes, leaving his seaside villa and his expensive automobiles.

'But why?' asks a friend in disbelief. 'You have everything!'

'Two reasons', says the man. 'First, the Government is in disarray. Its policies are deplorable, and it's leading the country to ruin.'

'But it will collapse soon', the friend reassures him, 'and the Labor Party will come back to power.'

'Yes', says the departing Israeli. 'That's the second reason.'

In the main, however, Israelis who do not (or cannot) leave the country consider those who do to be shirkers, seekers of the easy life, cowards, even figurative traitors. To them an emigrant is a *yored* ('one who descends'). And a *yored* is a pejorative word – in government circles, in social conversation, and even in the dictionary. It matters little that countless *yordim* (emigrants) have rushed back to fight and to die in each of Israel's wars.

Understandable as this negative reaction to *yeridah* may be in the light of Israel's tiny population and siege mentality, it is neither helpful nor effective. For Israel is a democracy and is caught in the trap of democracy. How can it prevent its own Jews from emigrating when it is constantly calling upon other countries – the USSR in particular – to let their Jews emigrate. Moreover, it has signed and ratified the Universal Declaration of Human Rights. Article 13 (2) of that document states: 'Everyone has the right to leave any country, including his own, and to return to his country.'

But not too many Israelis who have been away for more than four years have returned. As many as 500,000 have chosen not to return, and the problem has an American connection because about four-fifths of these emigrants live in the United States, principally in the New York and Los Angeles areas. Half of the American *yordim* are native-born Israelis, between 21 and 35 years of age, with a fairly good education. Because most of them feel guilty about having left Israel – a feeling that the overseas representatives of the Israeli government and the World Zionist Organization like to reinforce – American Jews do not quite know how to handle the situation, either personally or communally. As a result, most *yordim* in America, even if they have become American citizens, live suspended between three worlds: the American, the Jewish, and the Israeli.

Thinking Israelis in government and Zionist circles are beginning to realize that all but ignoring a half million potential supporters, when Israel needs all the friends abroad it can get, is foolish. They are trying to strike a balance between keeping closer contacts with their emigrants and not appearing to make emigration a too acceptable and attractive alternative to living in Israel. They are beginning to see that, while guiltmongering may make the folks at home feel better, it does not stop the determined 'guilty ones' from leaving anyway. In fact, with or without guilt feelings, about 10,000 Israelis are now coming to America each year, with smaller numbers going elsewhere.

Whether they like it or not, Israelis in Israel must adjust to the fact that 16 percent of their population at home now lives abroad. Put another way, Israel has its own group of 'overseas Chinese', and it ought to learn a valuable lesson from the Chinese. Imperial China, nationalist China, and Communist China all followed one policy: they never consigned their brethren abroad to purgatory and ostracism. Instead, they always sought to forge strong cultural, linguistic, and economic links with them in the hope that some day they, or their children, or their children's children would come back home. Over the centuries, many of them did. If Israel took a page from the Chinese book, it too might see its own emigrants or their offspring returning in the coming years and decades.

There is also an American connection with the saga of Jewish emigration from the Soviet Union. It was American Jews who started the initial agitation for Soviet Jewish emigration to Israel. It was the American government and Congress which continued the pressure, until, by 1968–70, the Kremlin began to let limited, but still large, numbers of Jews leave Russia. Between 1968 and December 1979 almost 250,000 of Russia's then Jewish population of about 3 million did leave. In the beginning all of them went to Israel. By 1973, however, 5 percent dropped out. By 1974 the drop-out rate was 20 percent. By 1979 it was 67 percent, mostly to Western countries, principally the United States. Aware of this trend, Soviet authorities now issue exit visas only to Jews with sponsors actually living in Israel. This means that any Soviet Jewish émigré who settles in the United States is automatically cutting off his relatives' chances of leaving Russia too.

Neshirah (or 'dropping out' in Hebrew) causes great anguish for Israelis and great dilemmas for Americans. The *noshrim* (drop-outs) not only do nothing to build up Israel's Jewish population, but when they opt to come to the United States, they are eligible for assistance from American Jewish organizations like HIAS (Hebrew Immigrant Aid Society) and the JDC (the American Jewish Joint Distribution Committee) as well as aid from the American government under the United States Refugee Relief Assistance Act. Israeli officials question the granting of refugee status to Soviet Jews who hold Israeli visas and are eligible for Israeli citizenship as soon as they set foot on Israeli soil. Arguments have erupted on both sides of the dropout issue, both within Israel and within the American Jewish community. Aryeh Dulzin, chairman of the executive of the World Zionist Organization, expressed the official Zionist and Israel position in the spring 1980 issue of the *United Synagogue Review*, an organ of the Conservative branch of Judaism in the United States. Calling the dropout rate 'a national calamity for Israel', Dulzin said :

> Soviet Jews are able to get to Vienna only because of the devotion and martyrdom of the Zionist activists in the Soviet Union and the direct involvement of the Israeli government. Once in Vienna, they are free men, and the Jewish people have only one *moral* commitment towards them, to get them to their homeland, Israel. There is no justification to finance their travel from one free country to another. The *noshrim* in Vienna hold valid Israeli papers and Israel is ready to receive them with open arms. Once in Israel, like any other Israeli, they are free to go wherever they want – but not at the expense of the Jewish people.
>
> Are we strengthening the Jewish people by bringing all those *noshrim* to the United States? . . . Let us not assist in the sad process of moving Jews from one *galut* [exile] to another.

In January 1980 an Israeli diplomat stationed in Washington put it more succinctly, when he told me : 'American Jews must not be so hospitable to *noshrim*.'

There are arguments on the other side of the issue. One example comes from Jack Greenfest, who lives in Jerusalem. Another example comes from Dr Michael Rapp, executive director of the Jewish Community Relations Council of Cincinnati, Ohio. In the 11–17 November 1979 issue of the *Jerusalem Post International Edition* Greenfest wrote, in a letter to the editor :

> The Soviet Jewish dropout issue not only bothers many of us now, but I suspect will continue to disturb us in the foreseeable future. As I see it, nothing can be done to stop Soviet Jews from going anywhere they wish. While we understandably wish our Jewish brethren to come here, what's so tragic about their going elsewhere? In fact when you think of it, it may be for the best.
>
> The gut aspect of Jewish emigration from the Soviet Union is to get them out of the Russian grip no matter how devious the method. For once they are out and breathing the air of freedom I am convinced they will set their goal as Israel, if not the present hopelessly lost generation, then their progeny. And even if

not, the State of Israel will at least have gained sympathizers.
Cheers for Hias [*sic*] and others who are doing their utmost
to comfort the Russian Jewish dropouts.

As for Dr Rapp, in a background paper called 'Problems in the
Soviet Jewry Movement: a local perspective', which he prepared
for the January 1980 plenary meetings of the National Jewish
Community Relations Advisory Council (NJCRAC), he wrote:

We are all aware that while Soviet Jews still leave on Israeli
visas, of the 50,000 Jews who left the Soviet Union during
1979, fully two-thirds settled in lands other than Israel. I am
at a loss as to why the American Jewish community is surprised
at this development. The emigrants of the late 1960s and early
1970s were essentially idealogues [*sic*] and/or activists who
perceived Israel as their ancestral land or religious Jews with
spiritual ties to Israel. The emigrants that Soviet officials are
allowing out today are those from urban industrial areas with a
limited Jewish background and with little, if any, Zionist
inclinations. In addition, one of the characteristics of Soviet
Jews in the United States today is that at least one-half of the
adults are highly trained and/or are university graduates.
Urbanism, lack of ideology, secularism, and high educational
levels are most assuredly not the social characteristics of those
who would be willing to emigrate to a land where the physical
demands upon them are great, while the opportunities for
upward mobility are restricted . . . Voluntary downward
mobility . . . is simply not the norm in human behavior. Nor
should this surprise us. Throughout most of the nineteenth
century, Russian Jews faced various forms of . . . discrimination
. . . Yet, [when they emigrated in mass numbers after the economically strangulating May Laws of 1882] . . . the majority . . .
migrated not to Palestine but to the rapidly expanding urban
frontiers of Central and Western Europe, Canada, Argentina,
and the United States. Why, then, should we expect contemporary Russian Jews to act in a manner unlike that of our grand-
parents whom we today commend for their courage and
foresight?
   It is this question that reflects the most divisive and yet most
irrelevant aspect of the entire movement . . . The most im-
portant goal of the Soviet Jewry Movement must be the saving
of Soviet Jewish lives and Soviet Jewish culture. To allow the

question of ultimate destination of Soviet emigrants to enter the discussion accomplishes nothing!

International law confers upon no sovereign state the duty to commit geographic or demographic suicide. But international reality makes geography and demography determinants in Israel's decisions about how to continue communal peace within itself and about how to find a secure peace with its neighbors. Israel has options. But some of them are not plausible, others are not possible, and all of them are dangerously problematic. Its basic choice is not between the bad and the good, or even between the bad and the bad. Instead, it is 'between the bad and the impossible', to quote retired Major-General Yehoshafat Harkabi, now a professor of international relations at Jerusalem's Hebrew University. A former chief of Israeli Military Intelligence and a former 'hawk' on the question of Palestinian self-determination, Harkabi has now concluded that 'Staying on the West Bank is impossible',[2] as did 57 percent of the retired senior military officers polled in 1974 by an Israeli sociologist. Fifty-two percent of the officers surveyed also saw the need for Palestinian self-determination.[3]

Whether or not the present and future leaders of Israel agree with Harkabi, they will not be able to ignore his international reputation as a great Arabist. Nor, when they ponder their geopolitical and demographic options, will they be able to ignore these four questions. First: 'if we former Palestinian Jews were unwilling to accept nonsovereign autonomy when the British ruled the area, why should the present Palestinian Arabs be willing to accept it from us when we are in charge – especially since those West Bank and Gaza Arabs who publicly accept Israeli statehood are prime candidates for terrorist assassination?' Secondly: 'does not the argument of many Jews that the Palestinian Arabs had their chance at statehood in 1947 but lost it forever when they rejected UN-sponsored partition open us up to the counterargument that when the Jews lost their sovereignty to the Romans in the year 70, they also lost the right to claim it again some 1900 years later?' Thirdly: 'if we continue to occupy territories containing some 1·2 million nonvoting, non-Israeli Arabs, what will this do to the democratic character of our state?' And fourthly, 'if we 3·2 million Jews annex the territories and grant citizenship to these million Arabs – even as we granted it to the 630,000 non-Jews already Israelis – what will this do to the Zionist and Jewish character of our state?'

13

Interlocking the United States and Israel

In order to help Israel come safely to grips with the four questions I have just raised – and to nudge the Arabs to accept the fact of Israel's legitimacy in the Middle East – the United States must make provision for the following:

- an American naval base in Haifa big enough to serve as the home port for the Mediterranean Sixth Fleet;
- smaller naval contingents in Eilat;
- air bases, personnel, and electronic listening stations in the Galilee and in the Negev;
- prepositioned land, sea, and air equipment in Israel for use either in Israel or elsewhere in the Middle East;
- the stationing in Israel of suitable numbers of American Army troops;
- insistence on a West Bank/Gaza Palestinian Arab state that, like neutralized Switzerland, will allow no foreign, especially great power, forces on its soil and that will eschew terrorism against Israel and make full and formal peace with it in return for Israel's agreement to go back to as many of the pre-1967 boundaries as are militarily defensible for its major population centers;
- American support for a Greater Jerusalem – perhaps including Bethlehem – that would be physically undivided but religiously and administratively cantonized along the lines of the Greater London Council or Metropolitan Toronto;
- a clear, binding, public, written, formal American mutual assistance treaty that says in effect that, if need be, America will use Israel as a staging area to meet other trouble spots in the Middle East and that as far as Israel's threatened existence

is concerned, that country, like the city of West Berlin, is on 'our side of the line' and that America will fight anyone – including the Russians and the Arabs – who crosses that line by force.

The elements of this all-or-nothing policy package are presented in full awareness of America's diminished (but not yet vanished) Vietnam trauma; the 1973–4 Arab oil boycott; the always inherent possibility of a Soviet-American military confrontation; my conviction that the best way to prevent such a confrontation is to convince the Russians that America is willing and able to confront them if forced to; the negative reaction by some segments of the American public at the mere stationing of American civilian technicians in the Sinai to monitor compliance with the Israeli-Egyptian disengagement accords; the depressing and distracting state of the United States economy; the inward-looking, neo-isolationist mood of many Americans today, and the belief of some of them that the Egyptian–Israeli peace treaty and the Palestine autonomy negotiations between Israel and Egypt are grounds for a smaller, not a greater, American military presence in the area. But the package is also presented in the belief that it contains great advantages to both the Americans and the Israelis, that neither country can maintain its vital interests in the region without the other, and that it offers a solution to the old Arab-Israel deadlock, which, once ended, will enable America, Israel, and moderate Arab states to face newer and more dangerous problems in the Middle East.

Like every set of political suggestions, this one is a mixture of facts, timing, assumptions, risks, and presumed advantages. It begins with what I consider to be the positions and reactions of the parties concerned. Moderate Arabs want an Israeli pullback to every inch of the pre-1967 borders and Israeli acceptance of the creation of a sovereign Palestinian Arab entity. Moderate Israelis have no wish for a long occupation or annexation of more than a million Arabs. But they, like their more uncompromising countrymen, remember that the old pre-Six-Day War frontiers brought them neither peace nor security in the two decades that they served as the *de facto* frontiers. This cannot be allowed to happen again, and America has no right to put Israel in a position where it might happen again.

Extremist Jews want an Israel without Palestine. Extremist Arabs want a Palestine without Israel. The Russians want influence and power in the area; yet they will probably accept whatever arrangements the Israelis and the Arabs accept even as they try to extract maximum credit for it. And the Americans would certainly accept the arrangements, especially if they removed a major cause of strategic instability in the Middle East.

The risks and advantages of the suggestions flow from their assumptions and from the facts. First, America has no naval and air bases on the southern shores of the Mediterranean. How long it will be able to get or keep them on the northern shores, in places like Portugal, Spain, Italy, Greece, and Turkey, is open to question. The same is true for the electronic listening stations in Turkey that now monitor the Soviet Union. Yet it is not questionable that American credibility abroad, badly shaken by Vietnam, Watergate, the fall of the Shah, the hostage crisis in Tehran, the destabilization of the Persian Gulf, the Russian invasion of Afghanistan, the Iraqi invasion of Iran, and increased Soviet influence in the Horn of Africa and the southern tips of Arabia, requires American shore-based naval and air facilities, as well as monitoring stations, in the entire region.

Second, there is a whole history of United States Israeli strategic and intelligence cooperation in the region. For instance, in 1966 Israeli intelligence persuaded an Iraqi pilot to fly a MIG-21 fighter to Israel. Within days, American technical specialists had their first look at this Soviet aircraft. During the 1967 war Israel tested American equipment and doctrine under battle conditions and reported back their findings and conclusions to their American allies. In that same war an Israeli-piloted American helicopter lifted out a fully operational SAM (surface-to-air missile) battery and sent it to the United States, giving American military men their first look at the weapon and their first fix on the radio frequencies it used. In the Six-Day War, Israel also captured the latest Soviet tanks, armored personnel carriers, and tank destroyer assault guns, some of which it made available to American specialists for study. In the so-called Israeli-Egyptian War of Attrition between 1967 and 1970, Israeli pilots on occasion engaged and shot down Russian-piloted aircraft with Egyptian markings. Again, they reported these encounters to the Americans, together with their assessment of Russian air tactics and pilot proficiency. In 1970, when Syrian tanks invaded Jordan and occupied the northern half of the country, only Israel's threat to intervene – a threat made at the behest of the United States – caused the Syrians to pull back to their own territory. In 1976 Israeli intelligence warned the leaders of Egypt and Saudi Arabia, through the American connection with all three countries, of planned coups against them. Throughout the current civil war in Lebanon the Israelis have been trying to help the Christians. In the process, they may have done more than any other country to keep alive the last sparks of Lebanese state sovereignty. Israel was also the first country to warn the Central Intelligence Agency of the impending upheaval in Iran and the threat to American interests, installations, and individuals there.

The Israelis were never consulted about how to rescue the American hostages in Tehran, and they were not informed beforehand about the attempt that did take place. Nevertheless they helped toward safeguarding the progress of the doomed operation. According to Jack Anderson, a widely read and respected nationally syndicated columnist, writing in the *Philadelphia Bulletin* of 26 August 1980 :

> There was a moment of high danger last April as American commandos, huddled in helicopters, rattled toward Iran. Hundreds of miles away, Israeli intelligence specialists were routinely monitoring radio communications. They picked up some suspicious transmissions and easily detected the hostage rescue operation.
>
> Acting quickly, they began sending out confusing signals to disguise the telltale US transmissions. Incredibly, the Americans had overlooked this elementary precaution. But fortunately the Israelis covered for them, or the ill-fated mission might have fared even worse.
>
> This has been reported by a Pentagon evaluation team in their secret findings. The report speculates that the Soviets, their surveillance capabilities unmatched, must have detected the signals. But thanks to the Israelis, the Soviets may not have interpreted the sounds correctly.

No wonder that retired Major-General George J. Keegan, former chief of United States Air Force Intelligence, has said that 'Israel's contribution [to the United States] was worth $1,000 for every dollar's worth of aid we have granted her' and that the 'military information we get from Israelis is worth billions'.[1] No wonder also that in January 1979 more than 170 retired American generals and admirals – including General Keegan sent an open letter to President Carter about Israel's strategic importance to the United States. They told the President that 'in a monumental conflict between the Soviet Union and the United States in the Middle

East, Israel alone might deter Soviet combat forces' intervention or prevent the completion of such deployment'. They urged him to recognize Israel's value as an ally since it could defend itself, thereby also defending American and Western interests against Russia's 'imperial objectives' which they described, in the paraphrased words of the *Times* as the 'neutralization of Western Europe, partly by denying it access to oil, the encirclement of China and the isolation of the United States'.[2]

Retired Admiral Elmo R. Zumwalt, a former chief of naval operations and a former member of the American Joint Chiefs of Staff, has been especially outspoken on behalf of Israel's strategic importance to the United States. He ends a letter to the *New York Times*, published on 2 October 1979, as follows :

> Thus US military planners rely on Israel's armed forces to counter Soviet proxy forces in the [Middle Eastern] region as well as to guarantee the US Sixth Fleet air superiority despite the Soviet Mediterranean fleet. A policy that justifies weakening Israel militarily . . . would damage US strategic policy while it endangers the survival of Israel.

Earlier he wrote :

> Israel's military value to the United States derives not only from its location adjacent to the oil-rich Persian Gulf region, at the junction of three continents, but also from the sophistication and prodigious efficiency of its defense forces. More important than either of these factors, however, is the reliability of the state of Israel as a comrade-in-arms on behalf of the essential interests of the Western world – interests which inevitably harmonize with those of the Jewish state as a result of the latter's dedication to the principles of democratic government.[3]

There are other reasons for interlocking the United States and Israel. An unequivocal public American commitment to Israel's secure survival, solidly backed by the stationing of American servicemen on Israeli soil, would prevent either the Arabs or the Israelis from starting a new war. These servicemen would not be United Nations observers, subject to what the Israelis believe are the anti-Israel whims of the Secretary-General and the General Assembly. They would be members of the armed forces of a superpower, and the Arabs, Israelis, and Russians would think very hard before they fired upon such forces. Furthermore, what I propose would let the Russians know exactly where America stands, and how far it is willing to go in regard to Israel. Knowing this, they would draw the proper Leninist conclusion : if after probing you find hard steel instead of soft flesh, you pull back and adjust. The Arabs would be compelled to make the same adjustment.

Even another oil boycott by Saudi Arabia, America's largest foreign supplier, is unlikely if the Americans place their firm military presence in Israel. Afraid of their own future after what happened to the pro-American Shah of Iran and his regime, the Saudis will publicly denounce such a presence. Privately, however, they will give thanks to Allah for his mercy and wisdom. In March 1981 the Saudi Foreign Minister, Prince Saud al-Faisal, told a meeting of Japanese and Western businessmen who had come to his country for a privately sponsored seminar : 'It is not by bombast or a show of strength that the Soviet Union will be stopped [in the Middle East], but by determination and the will to resist aggression.'[4] I do not believe that the Saudis will balk if part of that will and determination results from a stronger Israeli–American alliance.

As for the Israelis, even if they win fifty wars they can never be secure under the present circumstances. Yet if they lose only one war their existence may be over. Even if the Israelis were to win *every* future war against them, how would they be able to pay for them – in money, in weapons, and in lives? It is true that in the past the standard Israeli response to any suggestion of stationing American soldiers and facilities on their territory has been negative. More recently, however, the view that one hears in government circles may be summed up as follows : 'We will not push the Americans to put bases here, but if *they* ask us for permission to do so, we shall give it the most careful consideration and then most probably agree.' And to those in Israel who fear that an American military presence will diminish the quality of Jewish sovereignty, the answer can be made with a question : 'Are Japan, South Korea, West Germany, for instance, less sovereign because they have American military men and facilities on their soil?'

The Israelis cannot make Palestinian nationalism – the desire of the Palestinians for a state of their own – go away. But they must insist that if they accept a Palestinian Arab or Jordanian-Palestinian state to their east, then the United States will have to see to it that that state is not a PLO-dominated terrorist state, one which will use its new statehood as a way-station along the road to Israel's eventual elimination. If America will not or cannot guarantee this to Israel, then Israel will not and should not accept the new state or do anything by way of withdrawal to help in its creation. But Israelis will accept it – indeed they must accept it – if they are convinced that, like the Japanese, their own sovereign equality and territorial integrity are secure under an American military umbrella that will not be folded up and hidden away at the first sign of rain.

This brings us back to the Americans. They are the keystone in the whole structure. If they are really serious about their often-repeated fears of another Arab-Israel war, if they really want an Arab-Israel peace so that other important issues in the Middle East can be attended to, if they really want to counter the Russians in the area, particularly in the Persian Gulf and the Arabian Peninsula, then they will have to rearm and show the kind of will and determination generally that Prince Saud al-Faisal was talking about. With regard to Saudi Arabia, the Americans will have to pressure them to stop calling for holy wars against Israel and to stop bank-rolling PLO and other terrorist acts against Israel. With regard to Israel, the Americans will have to realize that because Israel has no other great power to turn to, because it cannot use the small power's ploy of trying to play one great power off against another, it is the most dependable ally that any country can possibly have. There are additional reasons for Israel's dependability: its proven military and technical capacity, its democratic value system, and the fact that should America ever have to use men and equipment that it has prepositioned for deployment either in Israel or elsewhere in the region, its legal right to do so will be protected not by the biopolitical longevity of whichever leader happens to be in power at the time but by Israel's institutionalized and functioning democracy.

Essentially, what I am suggesting is a robust quid pro quo between the largest democracy in North America and the only democracy in the Middle East. This mutual commitment ought to give Israel the courage to make another quid pro quo vis-a-vis the Palestinians and protect the minimal national interests of the three parties, if not indeed those of Jordan, Kuwait, Saudi Arabia, and other pro-American states as well. Finally, an American military guarantee of Israel's survival is the only way out of the latter's demographic dilemma and is the only logical extension of America's centuries-old commitment to both the Israel of religious beliefs and the Israel of living statehood.

Notes

Chapter 2

1 Quoted in Moshe Davis (ed.), *With Eyes Toward Zion* (New York: Arno Press, 1977), p. 9.
2 See Stanley F. Chyet (ed.), *The Event Is With the Lord* (Cincinnati, Ohio: American Jewish Archives, 1976).
3 Quoted in Davis, *With Eyes Toward Zion,* p. 11.
4 A photostat of the letter, together with a translation into English, is reprinted in Milton O. Gustafson, 'Records in the National Archives relating to America and the Holy Land', ibid., opposite p. 139.
5 Edmund Wilson, 'On first reading Genesis', in *Red, Black, Blond, and Olive* (New York: Oxford University Press, 1956), p. 387.
6 (Boston, Mass.: J. Gill, 1777). Samuel Langdon's sermon was published by Lamson & Ranlet in Exeter, New Hampshire, in 1788. Abiel Abbot's was published by Moore & Stebbins in Haverhill, Mass., in 1799.
7 Quoted in Truman Nelson, 'The Puritans of Massachusetts: from Egypt to the Promised Land', *Judaism*, vol. 16 (Spring, 1967), p. 206.
8 Reprinted in 1977 by Arno Press of New York in its seventy-two volume series, mostly of reprints, called 'America and the Holy Land'. The general editor of the series is Moshe Davis of the Hebrew University of Jerusalem.

Chapter 3

1 *Votes and Proceedings of the House of Delegates of Maryland, 1818 Session* (Annapolis, Md: John Green, 1819), p. 26.
2 Quoted in Davis, *With Eyes Toward Zion*, p. 19.
3 His account is in Orson Hyde, *A Voice From Jerusalem* (Boston, Mass.: Albert Morgan, 1842).
4 Quoted in Hertzel Fishman, *American Protestantism and a Jewish State* (Detroit, Mich.: Wayne State University Press, 1973), p. 21.
5 Quoted in George A. Smith *et al.*, *Correspondence of Palestine Tourists: Comprising a Series of Letters by George A. Smith, Lorenzo Snow, Paul A. Schettler, and Eliza R. Snow of Utah* (Salt Lake City, Utah: Deseret News Steam Printing Establishment, 1875), pp. 1–2.
6 Samuel S. Cox, *Orient Sun Beams, or From the Porte to the Pyramids, By Way of Palestine* (New York: Putnam, 1882), pp. 295–6.
7 Blackstone's memorial, the letter of transmittal accompanying it, and an article entitled 'May the United States intercede for the Jews?' are reprinted in *Christian Protagonists for Jewish Restoration* (New York: Arno Press, 1977), pp. 1–23.

Chapter 4

1 Quoted in Richard Libowitz, 'Some reactions to *Der Judenstaat* among English-speaking Jews in the United States', in Ronald A. Brauner (ed.), *Jewish Civilization: Essays and Studies,* vol. I (Philadelphia, Pa: Reconstructionist Rabbinical College, 1979), p. 138, n. 30.

2 This and the other references to Mordecai Manuel Noah are taken respectively from Benjamin L. Gordon, *New Judea: Jewish Life in Modern
   Palestine and Egypt* (Philadelphia, Pa: Julius H. Greenstone, 1919),
   p. xxi; Reuben Fink (ed.), *America and Palestine* (New York: American
   Zionist Emergency Council, 1944), p. 23; and M. M. Noah, 'Discourse on
   the restoration of the Jews' [1845], in *Call to America to Build Zion*
   (New York: Arno Press, 1977).
3 All quotations from Rabbi Hirsch are taken from Anita Libman Lebenson,
   'Zionism comes to Chicago', in Isadore S. Meyer (ed.), *Early History of
   Zionism in America* (New York: American Jewish Historical Society and
   Theodor Herzl Foundation, 1958), pp. 166 and 172.

Chapter 5

1 Quoted in 'Theodor Herzl', *Israel Digest*, vol. 5 (26 July 1954), p. 9.
2 Quoted in the *New York Times*, 15 September 1897, p. 6.
3 Except for those from the *New York Times*, all references and quotations
   relating to the early media responses to Herzl and Zionism are from Milton
   Plesur, 'The American press and Jewish restoration during the nineteenth
   century', in Meyer, *Early History of Zionism in America*, pp. 64–7.
4 Quoted in the *New York Times*, 17 August 1899, p. 2.
5 Quoted in ibid., 1 July 1907, p. 7.
6 Quoted in ibid., 23 August 1907, p. 6.
7 Quoted in ibid., 30 September 1907, p. 3.
8 Selig Adler, 'Backgrounds of American policy toward Zion', in Moshe
   Davis (ed.), *Israel: Its Role in Civilization* (New York: Jewish Theological
   Seminary of America, 1956), p. 273.
9 Quoted in the *New York Times*, 28 June 1915, p. 5.
10 Quoted in *Encyclopedia Judaica*, vol. IV (Jerusalem: Keter/Macmillan,
   1971), p. 1298.
11 Quoted in the *New York Times*, 23 April 1917, p. 8.
12 Quoted in ibid., 28 April 1917, p. 14.
13 This quotation is taken from ibid., 14 September 1918, p. 7.
14 Quoted in ibid., 22 December 1918, section 3, p. 10.
15 Quoted in ibid., 5 March 1919, p. 6.
16 Quoted in Lebenson, 'Zionism comes to Chicago', in Meyer, *Early History
   of Zionism in America*, pp. 169–70.
17 See *The Christian Century*, 13 December 1917, p. 718; 11 August 1927,
   p. 942; and 11 December 1929, p. 135.
18 Quoted in *Encyclopedia Judaica*, vol. IV, 131.
19 R. H. S. Crossman, 'Gentile Zionism and the Balfour Declaration', in
   Norman Podhoretz (ed.), *The Commentary Reader* (New York: Atheneum,
   1966), p. 293.
20 ibid., p. 292.
21 ibid.
22 Quoted in Jessie Sampter (ed.), *Modern Palestine* (New York: Hadassah,
   Women's Zionist Organization of America, 1933), p. 47. For President
   Wilson's thoughts about a Jewish *Commonwealth*, see Simon H. Rifkind
   et al., *The Basic Equities of the Palestine Problem* (New York: Hadassah,
   1947), p. 24.
23 Quoted in *The American War Congress and Zionism* (New York: Zionist
   Organization of America, 1919), p. 43. The quotations from the senators
   from Colorado, Maine, and Iowa are to be found on pp. 26–7, 33, and 38.

24 The quotations from the King–Crane Commission are taken from *Encyclopedia Judaica,* vol. XIII, pp. 30–1.
25 Quoted in Davis, *With Eyes Toward Zion,* pp. 243–4.
26 Quoted in Cyrus Adler and Aaron M. Margalith, *With Firmness in the Right: American Diplomatic Action Affecting Jews, 1840–1945* (New York: American Jewish Committee, 1946), p. 79.
27 Selig Adler, 'The Palestine question in the Wilson era', *Jewish Social Studies,* vol. 10 (October 1948), p. 334.

Chapter 6

1 Article 2 of the mandate for Palestine. The full text of the mandate is published as an appendix to Paul L. Hanna's *British Policy in Palestine* (Washington, DC: American Council on Public Affairs, 1942). This is the standard work on the subject, and I have relied heavily on it as well as on several conversations I had with Professor Hanna in Gainesville, Florida, in June 1979.
2 Quoted in Adler and Margalith, *With Firmness in the Right,* p. 84.
3 This quotation and the one by President Coolidge that follows are found in Reuben Fink (ed.), *America and Palestine* (New York: American Zionist Emergency Council, 1944), p. 88.
4 Quoted in W. D. Blanks, 'Herbert Hoover and the Holy Land: a preliminary study based upon documentary sources in the Hoover Presidential Library', in Davis, *With Eyes Toward Zion,* p. 165.
5 The plan was also published four years later in Hoover's book, *Addresses upon the American Road* (New York: Van Nostrand, 1949), pp. 16–17.
6 Both quotations are from my article 'The unmoved bystanders', *Congress Bi-Weekly,* vol. 35 (25 March 1968), pp. 19–22. This is a review of Arthur D. Morse, *While Six Million Died: A Chronicle of American Apathy* (New York: Random House, 1967).
7 Quoted in Morse, *While Six Million Died,* p. 210.
8 Quoted in Glick, 'The unmoved bystanders', p. 21.
9 Quoted in ibid.
10 The text of the 1939 White Paper (Cmd 6019) is printed in *Book of Documents Submitted to the General Assembly of the United Nations Relating to the Establishment of the National Home for the Jewish People* (New York: Jewish Agency for Palestine, 1947), pp. 100–11. The rest of this discussion and the quotations relating to it are from Julia E. Johnson (ed.), *Palestine: Jewish Homeland?,* vol. 18 of *The Reference Shelf* (New York: Wilson, 1946), p. 9; and Hanna, *British Policy in Palestine,* pp. 128, 134 and 152.
11 Fosdick's points are taken from *A Pilgrimage to Palestine* (New York: Macmillan, 1927), pp. 274–5, and 292–3.
12 All quotations of John Haynes Holmes are from his book *Palestine Today and Tomorrow: A Gentile's Survey of Zionism* (New York: Macmillan, 1929), pp. 81, 159–60.
13 Quoted in Mordecai M. Kaplan, *A New Zionism* (New York: Theodor Herzl Foundation, 1955), p. 144.
14 Quoted in Fink, *America and Palestine,* pp. 58–9.
15 Quoted in Adler and Margalith, *With Firmness in the Right,* p. 399.
16 Quoted in Adler and Margalith, *With Firmness in the Right,* pp. 397–8.
17 The *New York Times* of 2 March 1945, as quoted in Melvin I. Urofsky, *We Are One!* (Garden City, NY: Doubleday/Anchor, 1978), p. 62.

18   Johnson's, Rosenman's, and Baruch's reactions are all quoted in Urofsky, *We Are One!*

Chapter 7

1   According to an unnamed member of the 1946 Anglo-American Commission of Inquiry on Palestine who told this to Edwin Newman, the author *of Strictly Speaking* (Indianapolis, Ind., and New York: Bobbs-Merrill, 1974), p. 50.
2   Harry S. Truman, *Memoirs* (Garden City, NY: Doubleday, 1955), vol. II, p. 132.
3   ibid., p. 158.
4   ibid., p. 157.
5   Charles Herbert Stember and Others, *Jews in the Mind of America* (New York and London: Basic Books 1966), pp. 146–7.
6   ibid., pp. 175–8.
7   Quoted in Truman, *Memoirs*, vol. II, pp. 137–8.
8   ibid., p. 138; *New York Times*, 5 July 1945, p. 14; Zvi Ganin, *Truman, American Jewry, and Israel, 1945–1948* (New York and London: Holmes & Meier, 1979), p. 30.
9   Quoted in the *New York Times*, 3 October 1945, p. 4.
10   US Department of State, *Anglo-American Committee of Inquiry: Report to the United States Government and His Majesty's Government in the United Kingdom*, Publication 2536 (Washington, DC: Government Printing Office, 1946), p. vii.
11   Quoted in Ganin, *Truman, American Jewry, and Israel*, p. 55.
12   *Anglo-American Committee of Inquiry*, pp. 1–5, 8.
13   The full text of Attlee's statement, made on 1 May 1946, can be found in Jewish Agency, *Book of Documents Submitted to the General Assembly* . . . , pp. 267–8.
14   Quoted in the *New York Times*, 10 August 1946, p. 4.
15   Professor Hanna gave me a copy of the memorandum, which I include here with his permission.
16   Professor Hanna in a letter to me dated 22 July 1980. Bartley Crum, another member of the Anglo-American Committee, was also helpful. See his very pro-Zionist book *Behind the Silken Curtain* (New York: Simon & Schuster, 1947).
17   As quoted in the *New York Times*, 3 September 1947, p. 6.
18   Quoted in ibid., 9 October 1947, p. 12.
19   Unless otherwise indicated, my discussion on pressure tactics at the United Nations is taken from my book *Latin America and the Palestine Problem* (New York: Theodor Herzl Foundation, 1958), pp. 105–8.
20   Quoted in the international edition of the *Jerusalem Post*, 6–12 January 1980, p. 14, which quotes the newly released first volume of *Israel State Papers*.
21   Ganin, *Truman, American Jewry, and Israel*, p. 144.
22   Thomas J. Hamilton, 'Partition of Palestine', *Foreign Policy Records*, vol. 23 (15 February 1948), p. 291.
23   For the text of Ambassador Warren R. Austin's statement, see United Nations, Security Council, *Official Records, Third Year*, No. 46 (Lake Success, NY: United Nations, 1948), pp. 166–7.
24   Quoted in Ganin, *Truman, American Jewry, and Israel*, p. 162.
25   The first quotation, from an unnamed diplomat, is taken from former

Assistant Secretary of State Sumner Welles's book *We Need Not Fail* (Boston, Mass.: Houghton Mifflin, 1948), pp. 127–8. The second is by Dr Jorge García Granados of Guatemala, in United Nations, General Assembly, *Official Records, Second Special Session, First Committee* (Lake Success, NY: United Nations, 1948), p. 91.

26 Ganin, *Truman, American Jewry, and Israel*, p. 178.
27 Quoted in ibid., p. 187.
28 ibid., p. 189.
29 *Jews in the Mind of America*, p. 182.

Chapter 8

1 Unless otherwise noted, the information for this discussion, including quotations, comes from the *Reports* of the Conference of Presidents of Major American Jewish Organizations for the fiscal years ending 31 March 1977, 1978, and 1979, passim.
2 Quoted in an undated advertising brochure distributed by AIPAC at the 1980 meetings in Philadelphia of the National Jewish Community Relations Advisory Council.
3 Quoted in ibid.
4 Quoted in Stephen D. Isaacs, 'So who has the power?' *Present Tense*, vol. 1 (Summer 1974), p. 25.
5 *Philadelphia Bulletin*, 28 April 1980, p. A7.

Chapter 9

1 These facts and figures were supplied by Meir Dayan, consul for economic affairs in the Consulate-General of Israel in Philadelphia, during an interview with me on 13 October 1980, and by the Israeli Central Bureau of Statistics, as published in the *New York Times*, 30 December 1980, p. D7, and 12 October 1980, p. A17.
2 ibid., 10 July 1921, section II, p. 3. The figures for American private aid to Jewish Palestine from 1902 until 1935 come from ibid., 14 December 1924, section II, p. 2; 5 September 1926, p. 16; 28 January 1928, p. 4; 22 April 1929, p. 16; and 9 April 1930, p. 16.
3 United Jewish Appeal, *Annual Report, May 1980* (New York: UJA, 1980), p. 2.
4 The figures for the 1948–79 contributions by Americans through the United Jewish Appeal, the United Israel Appeal, and the Joint Distribution Committee were supplied by S. P. Goldberg, assistant director emeritus of the Council of Jewish Federations and Welfare Funds in New York in a letter to me, dated 9 October 1980, which was followed up by a conversation between us on 12 October 1980.
5 *My Life* (New York: Dell, 1976), p. 206.
6 Quoted in Urofsky, *We Are One!*, p. 162.
7 Meir, *My Life*, p. 206.
8 This information was supplied to me by Irving Kessler, executive vice-chairman of the United Israel Appeal, in an interview on 29 September 1980.
9 *Shnaton Statisti Le-yisreal, 1979* [Statistical Abstract of Israel, 1979],

(Jerusalem : Central Bureau of Statistics, 1980), p. 127. Unless otherwise indicated, all the statistics that follow come from this source.

10 According to my Temple University colleague, Dr Franklin H. Littell. Dr Littell, besides being professor and former chairman of the university's department of religion, is a Methodist minister, who is a member of President Carter's Commission on the Holocaust, president of the National Institute on the Holocaust, co-founder and chairman of Christians Concerned for Israel, and president of the National Christian Leadership Conference for Israel.

11 All of the information on Israel Bonds, including facts, figures, and quotations, are from a packet of materials put together and sent to me on 17 September 1980 by Betty Freeman, assistant executive director of the Greater Philadelphia branch of State of Israel Bonds.

12 *Jerusalem Post International Edition*, 5–11 October 1980, p. 9.

13 US Department of Commerce, *Statistical Abstract of the United States, 1979* (Washington, DC : Government Printing Office, 1979), p. 855; and *Jerusalem Post International Edition*, 12–18 October 1980, p. 12.

14 US *Statistical Abstract*, 1979, p. 857; US Agency for International Development, *US Overseas Loans and Grants and Assistance from International Organizations* (Washington, DC : Government Printing Office, 1980), p. 19; and *Jerusalem Post International Edition*, 12–18 October 1980.

15 ibid., 15–21 June 1980, p. 6.

16 Amiram Yarkoni, Modi'in Ezrachi's director, as quoted in ibid.

Chapter 10

1 Some of the ideas in this chapter I first developed in two scholarly papers and one article. The first paper, entitled 'Terrorism in the Middle East', was presented at the Oxford International Conference on Arms and Men, St John's College, Oxford University, in July 1978. The second paper, Arab terrorism and Israeli retaliation : some moral, psychological, and political reflections', was presented at the Conference on Moral Implications of Terrorism, sponsored by the University of California and the State University of New York, at UCLA, Los Angeles, in March 1979. The article is 'International terrorism and the aloof bystander', *Middle East Review: Special Reports*, December 1979, p. 1.

2 See the *New York Times*, 20 January 1979, p. A20.

Chapter 11

1 Quoted in Mordecai M. Kaplan, *A New Zionism* (New York : Theodor Herzl Foundation, 1955), pp. 96–7.

2 Theodor R. Mann, 'Israeli–American Jewish relationships', *Congress Monthly*, vol. 46 (April 1979), p. 10.

3 Kaplan, *A New Zionism*, pp. 151–3.

4 Unless otherwise indicated this discussion of religious differences is taken from my book *Between Israel and Death* (Harrisburg, Pa.: Stackpole Books, 1974), pp. 115–24. Copyright 1974 by Edward Bernard Glick.

5 The quotations from Rabbi Gittelsohn are taken from his article 'Any of our business?', *Jewish Frontier*, vol. 47 (May 1980), pp. 4–6, 20. They are reprinted with the permission of the publisher.

6   Resolution 61, in Jewish Agency, *Resolutions of the 29th Zionist Congress with a Summary of the Proceedings and the Composition of the Congress* (Jerusalem: Alpha Press, 1979), p. 48.
7   Quoted in Eliezer Whartman, 'Jerusalem Report', *Jewish Exponent*, 24 October 1980, p. 23. Whartman is the Jerusalem correspondent of the *Exponent*, and all quotations from his article are reprinted with the cooperation of the publisher. Copyright 1980, the *Jewish Exponent* of Philadelphia. Reprinted by permission.
8   Gittelsohn, 'Any of our business?', p. 5.
9   *Va'adat Hakhakirah: Milchemet Yom Hakippurim: Din Vekheshbon Khelki* [Investigating Commission: Yom Kippur War: Partial Report] (Jerusalem: 1 April 1974), see pp. 20–3, 25 and 27.
10 (Philadelphia, Pa: Jewish Publication Society of America, 1977). The three paragraphs that follow are composites of sentences and phrases from the book that appear on the rear dust jacket. The material is copyrighted by and used through the courtesy of the Jewish Publication Society of America.
11 *Jerusalem Post International Edition*, 19–25 August 1979, p. 23.
12 Maltbie Davenport Babcock, *Letters from Egypt and Palestine* (New York: Charles Scribner's Sons), p. 111.
13 *Encyclopedia Judaica*, vol. II, p. 634.
14 Quoted in Kaplan, *A New Zionism*, p. 96.

Chapter 12

1   These and all the other demographic statistics in this chapter come from the *Statistical Abstract of Israel* for 1977 and 1979; Coordinator of Government Operations in Judaea and Samaria, Gaza District, Sinai, Golan Heights, *A Twelve Year Survey, 1967–1979; Jewish Exponent* of Philadelphia, 1 February 1980; *Jerusalem Post International Edition*, 20–6 April 1980, p. 20, 3–9 August 1980, p. 5, and 14–20 September 1980, p. 5; *New York Times*, 5 June 1980, p. 3; Canadian Consulate in Philadelphia, 20 November 1980; and Drora Kass and Seymour Martin Lipset, 'Israelis in exile', *Commentary*, vol. 68 (November 1979), pp. 68–72.
2   Quoted in the *New York Times*, 5 May 1980, p. A19.
3   See Yoram Peri, 'Ofiyah Ha-idialogi shel Ha-elitah Hatzva'it Hayisraelit [The ideological character of the Israeli military elite]', *Medinah, Mimshal, Veyakhasim Bainle'umiim* [State, Government and International Relations], vol. 6 (Fall 1974) p. 147. Peri found that in general 'retired senior officers have expressed a greater need for territorial withdrawals and compromises than has the civilian population'.

Chapter 13

The title and some of the points in this chapter first appeared in an article published in the *New York Times* of 17 November 1977. © 1977 by The New York Times Company. Reprinted by permission.
1   Quoted in the *New York Times*, 3 February 1980, p. 22E.
2   ibid., 12 January 1979, p. A8.
3   From his introduction to Joseph A. Churba, *The Politics of Defeat* (New York and London: Cyrco Press, 1977), pp. 14–15.
4   Quoted in the *New York Times*, 9 March 1981, p. A7.

Selected Bibliography

I Books, Government Publications, and Special Studies

Adler, Cyrus, and Margalith, Aaron M., *With Firmness in the Right: American Diplomatic Action Affecting Jews, 1840–1945* (New York: American Jewish Committee, 1946).

Adler, Selig, Davis, Moshe, and Handy, Robert T., *America and Holy Land: A Colloquium* (Jerusalem : Institute of Contemporary Jewry of the Hebrew University of Jerusalem, 1972).

The American Republic and Ancient Israel (New York : Arno Press, 1977).

The American War Congress and Zionism (New York : Zionist Organization of America, 1919).

Babcock, Maltbie Davenport, *Letters from Egypt and Palestine* (New York : Charles Scribner's Sons, 1902).

Bell, Marion L., *Crusade in the City: Revivalism in Nineteenth Century Philadelphia* (Lewisburg, Pa : Bucknell University Press, 1977).

Berle, Adolph Augustus, *The World Significance of a Jewish State* (New York : Mitchell Kennerley, 1918).

Book of Documents Submitted to the General Assembly of the United Nations Relating to the Establishment of the National Home for the Jewish People (New York : Jewish Agency for Palestine, 1947).

Call to America to Build Zion (New York : Arno Press, 1977).

Christian Protagonists for Jewish Restoration (New York : Arno Press, 1977).

Churba, Joseph, *The Politics of Defeat* (New York and London: Cyrco Press, 1977).

Conference of Presidents of Major American Jewish Organizations, *Reports* (New York : Conference of Presidents, 1977–9).

Coordinator of Government Operations in Judaea and Samaria, Gaza District, Sinai, and Golan Heights, *A Twelve Year Survey, 1967–1979* (Tel-Aviv : Ministry of Defense, October 1979).

Crum, Bartley C., *Behind the Silken Curtain: A Personal Account of Anglo-American Diplomacy in Palestine and the Middle East* (New York : Simon & Schuster, 1947).

Davis, Moshe (ed.), *Israel: Its Role in Civilization* (New York : Jewish Theological Seminary of America, 1956).

Davis, Moshe (ed.), *With Eyes Toward Zion* (New York : Arno Press, 1977).

Davis, Moshe (ed.), *World Jewry and the State of Israel* (New York : Arno Press, 1977).

Dupuy, Trevor N., *Elusive Victory: The Arab-Israeli Wars, 1947–1974* (New York : Harper & Row, 1978).

Elath, Eliahu, *Zionism at the UN: A Diary of the First Days* (Philadelphia, Pa : Jewish Publication Society of America, 1976).

Elazar, Daniel J., *Community and Polity: The Organizational Dynamics of American Jewry* (Philadelphia, Pa : Jewish Publication Society of America, 1976).

Elizur, Yuval, and Salpeter, Eliahu, *Who Rules Israel?* (New York : Harper & Row, 1973).

Fink, Reuben (ed.), *America and Palestine* (New York : American Zionist Emergency Council, 1944).

Fishman, Hertzel, *American Protestantism and a Jewish State* (Detroit, Mich. : Wayne State University Press, 1973).

Fosdick, Harry Emerson, *A Pilgrimage to Palestine* (New York : Macmillan, 1927).

Ganin, Zvi, *Truman, American Jewry, and Israel, 1945–1948* (New York and London : Holmes & Meier, 1979).

García Granados, Jorge, *The Birth of Israel: The Drama as I Saw It* (New York : Knopf, 1948).

Glick, Edward Bernard, *Latin America and the Palestine Problem* (New York : Theodor Herzl Foundation, 1958).

Glick, Edward Bernard, *Between Israel and Death* (Harrisburg, Pa : Stackpole Books, 1974).

Glick, Edward Bernard, *Israel and Her Army* (New York : Labor Zionist Alliance, 1977).

Gordon, Benjamin L., *New Judea: Jewish Life in Modern Palestine and Egypt* (Philadelphia, Pa : Julius H. Greenstone, 1919).

Halkin, Hillel, *Letters to an American Jewish Friend* (Philadelphia, Pa : Jewish Publication Society of America, 1977).

Hanna, Paul L., *British Policy in Palestine* (Washington, DC : American Council on Public Affairs, 1942).

Herzl, Theodor, *Der Judenstaat: Versuch einer Modernen Lösang der Judenfrase* (Vienna : Breitenstein, 1896).

Himmelfarb, Milton, and Singer, David (eds.), *American Jewish Year Book 1980* (New York and Philadelphia, Pa : American Jewish Committee and the Jewish Publication Society of America, 1979).

Hoffer, Eric, *Before the Sabbath* (New York : Harper & Row, 1979).

Holmes, John Haynes, *Palestine Today and Tomorrow: A Gentile's Survey of Zionism* (New York : Macmillan, 1929).

Holy Land Missions and Missionaries (New York : Arno Press, 1977).

Hoover, Herbert, *Addresses upon the American Road* (New York : Van Nostrand, 1949).

Jervis, David T., 'American attitudes toward a Jewish state, 1620–1948', unpublished graduate paper, Temple University, Philadelphia, Pa, 1979.

Jewish Agency, *Resolutions of the 29th Zionist Congress with a Summary of the Proceedings and the Composition of the Congress* (Jerusalem : Alpha Press, 1979).

Kaplan, Mordecai M., *A New Zionism* (New York : Theodor Herzl Foundation, 1955).

Lapide, P. E., *A Century of US Aliya* (Jerusalem : Association of Americans and Canadians in Israel, 1961).

Liebman, Charles S., *The Ambivalent American Jew* (Philadelphia, Pa : Jewish Publication Society of America, 1976).

Lipsky, Louis, *Memoirs in Profile* (Philadelphia, Pa : Jewish Publication Society of America, 1975).

Liptzin, Sol, *Generation of Decision: Jewish Rejuvenation in America* (New York : Bloch, 1958).

Lowdermilk, Walter Clay, *Palestine: Land of Promise* (London : Gollancz, 1944).

Maslow, Will, *The Structure and Functioning of the American Jewish Community* (New York : American Jewish Congress and the American Section of the World Jewish Congress, 1974).

Meir, Golda, *My Life* (New York : Dell, 1976).

Meyer, Isadore S. (ed.), *Early History of Zionism in America* (New York : American Jewish Historical Society and Theodor Herzl Foundation, 1958).

Morse, Arthur D., *While Six Million Died: A Chronicle of American Apathy* (New York : Random House, 1967).

Neusner, Jacob, *American Judaism* (Englewood Cliffs, NJ : Prentice-Hall, 1972).

Polier, Justine Wise, and Wise, James Waterman (eds.), *The Personal Letters of Stephen Wise* (Boston, Mass. : Beacon Press, 1956).

Sampter, Jessie (ed.), *Modern Palestine* (New York : Hadassah, Women's Zionist Organization of America, 1933).

Silver, Abba Hillel, *Vision and Victory* (New York : Zionist Organization of America, 1949).

Sklare, Marshall (ed.), *The Jews: Social Patterns of an American Group* (New York : The Free Press, 1958).

Smith, George A., *et al.*, *Correspondence of Palestine Tourists* (Salt Lake City, Utah : Deseret News Steam Printing Establishment, 1875).

Statistical Abstract of Israel (Jerusalem : Central Bureau of Statistics, 1977–80).

Stember, Charles Herbert, and Others, *Jews in the Mind of America* (New York and London : Basic Books, 1966).

Truman, Harry S., *Memoirs* (Garden City, NY : Doubleday, 1955).

Urofsky, Melvin I., *We Are One!* (Garden City, NY : Doubleday/ Anchor, 1978).

US Agency for International Development, *US Overseas Loans and Grants and Assistance from International Organizations* (Washington, DC : Government Printing Office, 1980).

US Department of Commerce, *Statistical Abstract of the United States, 1979* (Washington, DC : Government Printing Office, 1979).

US Department of State, *Anglo-American Committee of Inquiry: Report to the United States Government and His Majesty's Government in the United Kingdom*, Publication 2536, (Washington, DC : Government Printing Office, 1946).

Welles, Sumner, *We Need Not Fail* (Boston, Mass. : Houghton Mifflin, 1948).

Wilson, Evan M., *Decision on Palestine* (Stamford, Calif. : Hoover Institution Press, 1980).

Wise, Stephen, *Challenging Years* (New York : Putnam, 1949).

II Articles

Adler, Selig, 'The Palestine question in the Wilson era', *Jewish Social Studies*, vol. 10 (October 1948), pp. 303–34.

Blanks, W. D., 'Herbert Hoover and the Holy Land : a preliminary study based upon documentary sources in the Hoover Presidential Library', in Moshe Davis (ed.), *With Eyes Toward Zion*, pp. 163–72.

Crossman, R. H. S., 'Gentile Zionism and the Balfour Declaration', in Norman Podhoretz (ed.), *The Commentary Reader* (New York : Atheneum, 1966), pp. 284–94.

Davis, Moshe, 'The Holy Land idea in American spiritual history', in his *With Eyes Toward Zion*, pp. 3–33.

Gittelsohn, Roland B., 'Any of our business?' *Jewish Frontier*, vol. 47 (May 1980), pp. 4–6, 20.

Glick, Edward Bernard, 'Jews and judíos', *Jewish Frontier*, vol. 34 (December 1967), pp. 11–14.

Glick, Edward Bernard, 'Why Israel should selectively boycott the United Nations', *Jewish Frontier*, vol. 39 (November 1972), pp. 15–17.

Glick, Edward Bernard, 'The Israeli Officer Corps after the Yom Kippur War', *International Perspectives*, July/August 1975, pp. 28–33.

Glick, Edward Bernard, 'Interlocking the US and Israel', *New York Times*, 17 November 1977, p. A25.

Glick, Edward Bernard, 'Why not sock it to OPEC?' *Philadelphia Bulletin*, 13 March 1979, p. A7.

Glick, Edward Bernard, 'International terrorism and the aloof bystander', *Middle East Review: Special Reports*, December 1979, p. 1.

Glick, Edward Bernard, 'Apathy causes terrorism to spread', *Philadelphia Bulletin*, 21 December 1979, p. A15.

Gustafson, Milton O., 'Records in the National Archives relating to America and the Holy Land', in Moshe Davis (ed.), *With Eyes Toward Zion*, pp. 129–58.

Gutmann, Emanuel, 'Religion and its role in national integration in Israel', *Middle East Review*, vol. 12 (Fall 1979), pp. 31–6.

Hamilton, Thomas J., 'Partition of Palestine', *Foreign Policy Records*, vol. 23 (15 February 1948), pp. 286–95.

Handy, Robert T., 'Sources for understanding American Christian attitudes toward the Holy Land, 1800–1950', in Moshe Davis (ed.), *With Eyes Toward Zion*, pp. 34–56.

Horowitz, Irving Louis, 'The politics of centrism: Jews and the 1980 elections', *Jerusalem Letter: Viewpoints*, vol. 13 (16 May 1980), pp. 1–16.

Isaacs, Stephen D., 'So who has the power?', *Present Tense*, vol. 1 (Summer 1974), pp. 24–8.

Kass, Drora, and Lipset, Seymour Martin, 'Israelis in exile', *Commentary*, vol. 68 (November 1979), pp. 68–72.

Kass, Drora, and Lipset, Seymour Martin, 'America's new wave of Jewish immigrants', *New York Times Magazine*, 7 December 1980, pp. 44, 100–1, 110, 112, 114, 116–18.

Libowitz, Richard, 'Some reactions to *Der Judenstaat* among English-speaking Jews in the United States', in Ronald A. Brauner (ed.), *Jewish Civilization: Essays and Studies*, vol. I (Philadelphia, Pa: Reconstructionist Rabbinical College, 1979), pp. 123–40.

Lowdermilk, Walter C., 'The Eleventh Commandment', *The Christian Rural Fellowship Bulletin*, no. 74 (September 1942), n.p.

Mann, Theodore R., 'Israeli–American Jewish relationships', *Congress Monthly*, vol. 46 (April 1979), 9–11.

Moskin, J. Robert, 'The Diaspora is alive and kicking', *Present Tense*, vol. 5 (Summer 1978), 6–7.

Nathan, Joan, 'So for this you left Israel?', *Present Tense*, vol. 1 (Spring 1974), 47–50.

Stern, Sol, 'Menachem Begin vs. the Jewish lobby', *New York*, 24 April 1978, pp. 59–63.

Index

Abbot, A. 23, 24
Adams, J. 26
Agranat Commission 137
aid *see* economic aid; foreign aid;
    military aid
Allenby, E. 56
Alnight, W. F. 68
American Christian Palestine Com-
    mittee 68, 86
American Council for Judaism 56, 68
American Israel Public Affairs Com-
    mittee 96, 102
American Jewish Alternatives to
    Zionism 69–70
American Jews 31–2, 45–6, 52, 96–7,
    125–7
    and anti-Zionism 42, 44, 48
    and Zionism 35–7, 43, 46–7, 138–9
    'drop-outs' 148–9
    lobbying power 95, 98–104
    voting influence 104–6
American Palestine Committee 67–8
Anderson, J. 155
Anglo-American Committee of Inquiry
    78
    members 79
    recommendations 80–1
    terms of reference 79
anti-Semitism 35–6, 38, 60
anti-Zionism
    and the American press 39–42
    Christian 49–50
    Jewish 35–6, 42, 44, 47–8
    organisations 69–70
Arab people
    conflict with Jews 74, 88–9
    in Israel 145
    in Palestine 62–3, 83, 151
    resettlement in Iraq plan 58
assassination 121
Association of Rabbis in Israel 135–6
Atkinson, H. A. 68, 90
Attlee, C. 78, 81
Aydelotte, F. 79

Babcock, M. D. 142
Balfour, A. J. 50, 51

Balfour Declaration 50–1, 52–3, 63
Begin, M. 100, 124
    National Military Organisation 74
Ben-Shalom, Z. 131
Berkowitz, H. 48
Berle, A. A. 49
Bevin, E. 79
Biltmore Conference 69
Blackstone, W. E. 28–30, 36–7, 49
Bradford, W. 19–20
Brandeis, L. D. 45–6, 51
Buxton, F. W. 79

Carigal, R. H. I. 20
Carter, J. 100, 104, 140
Christian Council on Palestine 68
Conference of Presidents of Major
    American Jewish Organisations
    96, 97–101
Coolidge, C. 58
Cox, S. 28
Crane, C. R. 53
Cresson, W. 27
Crick, W. P. 79
Crossman, R. H. S. 51, 80
Crum, B. C. 79, 90
Cuba
    and Jewish refugees 61
    vote against partition 88
Cummins, A. B. 53

Dayan, M. 124
Diaspora Jews 88, 126, 138, 140
    numerical importance 143
    see also American Jews
Dubov, M. H. 21

economic aid
    to Israel 109–12
    to Palestine 107–9
Eisenhower, D. D. 78

Ford, G. 104
foreign aid
    importance to Israel 107, 116
Fosdick, H. E. 65
Friedenwald, H. 43

Gittelsohn, R. B. 132, 135
Gordon, W. 23, 24
Goren, S. 136–7
Grady, H. F. 81
Great Britain
  Declaration of Sympathy with Zionism 50–1
  negotiations with America over Palestine 78–84
  Palestine endorsement 47
  Palestine rule 56, 62–3, 73–4, 78
Green, W. 67

Hadassah 69
Haldeman, I. M. 40
Hale, F. 52–3
Hanna, P. 82–4
Harding, W. G. 57
Harkabi, Y. 151
Harrison, E. G. 77–8
Harvard University 20
Hay, J. 21
Hebrew language
  and colonial America 20–2
  as required subject for university 20
Henderson, L. 90
Herzl, T. 36, 38, 41–2
Herzog, C. 98
Hildring, J. 87–8
Hirsch, E. G. 36
Hitler, A. 60, 61
Holmes, J. H. 65, 68
Hoover, H. 58–9
House, E. 51
Humphrey, H. 104
Hutcheson, J. C. 79
Hyde, O. 26

immigration
  aid organisations 148
  'drop-outs' problem 148–50
  the First 25
  illegal 74
  into Israel 139, 145–6
  into Palestine 76–80, 142–3
Iran
  and American hostages 155
Iraq
  Hoover Plan for resettling Palestinian Arabs 58–9
Israel 35, 91
  aid through Bonds Organisation 112–15
  and the Orthodox establishment 128–9, 132–6
  attitude to terrorism 117–23
  demography 144–5
  economy 107
  emigrants 146–7
  immigrants 139, 145–6
  military service 129–32
  relationship with USA 95, 152–8
  strategic importance 155–7
  voluntary donations to 108–12
  see also Zionism
Israel Labor Party 134–5
Israel, M. B. see Cresson, W.
Israeli Jews 145
  and ultra-Orthodox domination 128–36
  relationship with Diaspora Jews 126–9, 140–1

Jacobson, E. 91
Jewish National Fund 108
Jewish people 124–5
  of the Diaspora 88, 126, 138, 143
  see also American Jews; Israeli Jews; Judaism; Palestinian Jews
Johnson, H. 20
Johnson, L. B. 106
Judaism see Orthodox Judaism; Reconstructionist Judaism; Reform Judaism

Kaplan, M. M. 127–8
Keegan, G. J. 155–6
Kennedy, J. F. 104
kibbutz
  early conceptions of 27, 33
King, H. C. 53
Kirchway, F. 90
Kissinger, H. 99–100

Labor Zionist Alliance 134–5
Labor Zionists 69
Langdon, S. 23, 24
League of Nations
  mandates on Palestine 57
  see also United Nations
Leeser, I. 34–5
Legget, F. 79
Lewisohn, A. 46–7
Lodge, H. C. 51–2
Lowdermilk, W. C. 66–7

McDonald, J. G. 79
McGovern, G. 104
McNary, C. F. 67
Manningham-Buller, R. E. 79
Meir, G. 109–10, 130
Mexico
    condemnation of Israeli raid on
        Entebbe 99
military aid
    to Israel 115–16
military service
    in Israel 129–32
Mizrachi 69
Mor, O. 131
Moran, F. J. C. 40
Morgenthau, H. 48
Mormon Church 21, 26
Morrison, *Lord* 80, 81
Morrison-Grady Scheme 81–2
Murray, J. E. 78
Murray, P. 90

National Jewish Community Relations
    Advisory Council 96, 150
Niebuhr, R. 68–9
Nixon, R. M. 104, 106
Noah, M. M. 32–4

Ochs, A. S. 42, 48
Orthodox Judaism 127–9, 132–6

Palestine
    American support for Jewish 28–30,
        31–5, 49, 51–3, 56–8, 67–8, 90–2
    British rule 56, 62–3, 73–4, 78
    Independence 85, 145
    Jewish immigration to 25–7, 74, 76,
        142
    research studies on 53–4, 76–7
    UN partition resolution 74–5, 87–8
    UN Special Committee 85–6
    voluntary economic support for
        107–9
    White Paper on 63–4
Palestine Foundation Fund 108
Palestine National Loan Fund 109
Palestinian Jews 73–4, 76
    violence with Arabs 88–9
partition
    American view of 87–92
    plans 56, 63
    UN resolution 74–5, 87–8
patriotism
    of Zionist Jews 43–4

Patton, J. G. 90
Peace Now 138
Peel Commission 62–3
Phillips, W. 79
Phillipson, D. 47–8
Pilgrims 19–20
Poling, D. A. 68
politics
    and American Jewish lobby 95–103
    and the Middle East problem 152–8
    and Zionism 24, 30, 47–8, 57, 60,
        64–5, 70
    effect of Jewish vote in America
        104–6
population
    patterns in Israel 144–6
press
    and anti-Zionism 39–42
    and pro-Palestine petition 30

Rapp. M. 149–51
Reconstructionist Judaism 127
Reform Judaism 35, 42, 48, 133–4
Rieger, E. 124
Roche, J. 106
Roosevelt, F. D. 59–61, 64–5, 70–2,
    104, 105
Rosedale, S. W. 48

al-Sadat, A. 100
Saudi Arabia
    and American-Israeli relations 157,
        158
Schechter, S. 44
Schiff, J. H. 44, 47
Schroeder, G. 61–2
Senior, M. 48
Shalom Achshav 138
Silver, A. H. 106
Singleton, J. 79
Smith, E. 24, 25
Smith, J. 21, 26
Soviet Union
    Jewish emigration 148, 149–50
State of Israel Bonds Organisation
    112–15, 136
Stettinus, E. R. 74
Stiles, E. 20
survey research
    on setting up a Jewish state 76–7
Syria
    view of Palestine 32

Taft, R. A. 68, 106

Taft, W. H. 50
terrorism 117
  and retaliation 121-3
  Israeli view of 118-21
Thackery, T. O. 90
Thomas, C. S. 52
Thompson, D. 67
Tillich, P. 68
tourism
  importance to Israel 111
Trueman, H. S. 72, 73-81, 84, 89-92,
  105-6

Union of Soviet Socialist Republics
  see Soviet Union
unions
  and purchase of Israel bonds 113-15
United Israel Appeal 109, 110
United Jewish Appeal 109, 111
United Nations
  admission of Israel 15, 91
  and partition of Palestine 56, 74-5,
  85
  pressure and the partition vote 75,
  87-8
  Special Committee on Palestine
  85-6
United States of America
  and World War II refugees 60-2
  early links with Israel 19, 22-4
  hostages in Iran rescue attempt 155
  integration of Jewish immigrants
  45, 147-9
  joint negotiations with Britain over
  Palestine 78-84
  military aid to Israel 115-16
  Presidential elections and Jewish
  vote 104-6
  pro-Palestine moves 28-30, 51-3,
  57-8, 67-8
  research studies on Palestine 53-4,
  76-7

strategic policy in Middle East
  152-8
support for Palestine immigration
  25-8, 54, 76-8
view on Palestine partition 87-92
voluntary fundraising for Israel
  108-12
universities
  and Hebrew language 20, 22

Wagner, R. F. 67, 68
Weizmann, C. 51, 75, 91
Whartman, E. 136
White Paper on Palestine 63-4
Wilson, E. 21-2
Wilson, W. 48, 50, 51, 53, 54-5
Wise, I. M. 42
Wise, S. S. 51
women
  and Israeli national service 130-2
  see also Hadassah
World War I
  effect on American Zionism 44,
  46-7
World War II 56, 57, 59-60
World Zionist Organisation 42, 133
  Congresses 37, 138

Yishuv see Palestinian Jews
Young, A. 140
Young, B. 26

Ze'ira, E. 137
Zionism 35-7, 38-43, 46-55
  and American policy 56-62, 64-72
  and racism 98-9
  Christian support for 25-8, 49,
  65-8, 115-16
  effect of World War I 44, 46-7
  weakness of 43-4
Zionist Organisation of America 69

K1